Network Marketing Perfect Niche: Baby Boomers

How to Recruit Boomers into your MLM Business

David Williams

Network Marketing Perfect Niche: Baby Boomers

ISBN 978-1514396254

Table of Contents

Niche Marketing Magic for Networkers – What you have never been taught

Before we get into specifically understanding the boomers market, I want to give you some powerful marketing concepts that will make you a master marketer in any niche. I'll break this down over two chapters.

It seems people really don't 'get' niche marketing or target marketing. They have been brain-washed into believing the giant lie that 'everyone is a prospect'.

Years ago, when I got started in this industry, nobody spoke of niche marketing, what so ever.

My sponsor quit a few days after I joined. Then his sponsor quit and so did the next. I had to ask my questions to the only upline I could find.

He was a fellow who knew the business reasonably well and his wife knew all about the products. Between the two I was able to get my questions answered.

I asked, "What kind of people do the best in this industry, in our company, and who should I be looking for?"

He said, "As far as I'm concerned, anybody who can fog up a mirror. Talk to everybody you know."

I replied, "Okay, that's what you say at the meetings, but really, who are the best people? Tell me. Don't hide this information."

He had no clue. He thought, "What are you talking about? Just anybody who wants to make money."

That's everybody I said.

He said, "Yeah, everybody. Everybody wants to make money." I went away a bit despondent, quite honestly. I thought this is not logical and I'm a logical person. I remember thinking this doesn't make sense. I remember him saying, "If you throw enough spaghetti against the wall, some will stick."

Okay, there's a certain logic to that and I used to think of it as shotgun recruiting. If you shoot a shotgun at a group of people, you're going to hit some. Shoot and hope for the best. An example of this would be placing an ad in 'The Socialist Weekly.' Sure, someone reading it may be a secret capitalist but, it's unlikely.

If you have unlimited time and an unlimited budget, it will work eventually.

I thought using a rifle would make more sense. It's a bad analogy, shooting people, but you understand my point. His point was if you use a rifle and you miss, you get nobody. I felt it was better to take a little more time and get it right - fish in a pond of hungry fish, not in an ocean.

I figured I was the right person for this business and there must be more like me!

He had another team leader who had made some good numbers in the past, but his team just died out. He said this to our sponsor: "Look, you've been in this business for four years and you kept me in. I followed and you never found anybody that was any good."

He said, "Well, what about David?"

He answered, "David was a fluke."

I was a fluke because I was looking for a business opportunity. I searched the newspapers until I saw ads that said 'earn 10 grand a month'. I called the first ad and the guy who answered was too busy to talk to me. So, I called the next ad and it turned out to be someone who paid for the ad, but did nothing else. However, I was told there was a meeting the next night and I went.

I realized this is not normal. This is not average. That's not the way it's going to be because I also saw all the other people who arrived from that ad. Not really good quality.

I did run a lot of those ads that first year because I wanted to try them. I learned a lot about the business and doing presentations because I was doing presentations 4 nights a week.

Although, I soon realized what didn't work and I was spinning my wheels.

That was my first year, tossing spaghetti against the wall and holding up most of it with my hands!

I did try everything my upline said, but I ended up recruiting a lot of low-life's and people who were just not interested in working, but needed money.

How many months did I spend pushing and motivating that group? Some I had to teach how to dress, tell them to bathe before coming to meetings, and to brush their teeth before prospecting.

I was motivating because I did believe, and still do, that anyone can succeed and change.

The problem was that I wanted them to change and succeed more than they did.

Now, this lesson really hit home for me when I started 'recruiting up.'

When you recruit up you don't need to teach anyone to brush their teeth before attending meetings or to dress right, but if a well-to-do person has no real interest in success, you still can't 'motivate' them to 'go for it'.

I realized later in life, after learning and understanding the psychology of network marketing, that people who need money and people who desire - and are willing to work for money are two different groups. In the beginning I wasn't mature enough in my understanding to separate the two.

It was a huge amount of heartache. I think every single one of us goes through that unless we've already somehow been through this in another industry like sales or social work!

Targeting the right people!

When we talk about looking at our markets and targeting, we need to really understand this before we make that decision to do niche marketing.

If you go after horizontal markets, it's a lot tougher.

What's a horizontal market?

Well, for example, it's if I ask you, "Who's the market for your opportunity?"

And you say, "Everybody who wants to make money, David. Everybody wants to make money. That's our target market."

That tells me you have marketing immaturity because that is not your market. It shows a lack of critical thinking. One of Napoleon Hill's 17 success principles, often attacked by well-meaning upline sponsors everywhere is, 'don't reinvent the wheel').

Look, everyone wants more money. Your opportunity offers more money, but only IF a person is willing to sacrifice their time, their energy, a little money, enjoys our type of business, and WANTS to.

So, now the real market is cut down from 100% of people. All people, whether rich, filthy rich, or poor want more money. NEVER think anyone doesn't. However, only 20% are willing to sacrifice their time, energy, and some money to do something about it.

From that 20%, only some are suitable for networking. Others are going to choose second jobs, investing, day-trading, crafting, small traditional business, online business, etc.... Not everyone wants or is really a target for our marketing dollar.

Notice what I just wrote.

I did not say that the entire 20% are not potential distributors. They are, but not all of them are worthy of our marketing time and money.

Niche marketing is all about probabilities.

By drilling down into identifiable and suitable markets, we don't waste our time and money because the probability is stronger for us if we focus on a niche market on which it makes sense to spend our efforts.

So, let's not think pie-in-the-sky 'everyone is our market' because only a fool would choose 'everyone' as their niche.

Get rich in a niche

In fact, when a prospect asks you, 'what's the best market?' and you say 'anyone,' it sounds scammy.

When I was in the water filter business and someone asked that question we were trained to pause, look contemplative, and then say 'anyone that drinks water.' It's a nice sound bite but so immature, I felt dirty when I said it. It may sound clever but it shows a lack of critical thinking.

If you are in a skin-care company and you tell your team that 'anyone with skin' is a prospect, it's just as bad.

There are millions and millions of people who don't give a fig about water. I've met people who never drink water on its own. There are some who only drink soda, pop, or coffee. In the time of Henry the 8th, folks did not drink water because it was foul. They drank weak beer because the alcohol killed the germs.

What about skin care? Go into a pub and do a survey about the importance of keeping your face and skin healthy. Then go into a spa and conduct the same survey.

After that survey would you rather target market customers of pubs or customers of spas?

There are always outliers who care about skin care and hang out in pups all day long playing pool. There must be a person who goes to a spa and does not care about their skin, but I believe in probabilities.

How to double your bet with probabilities

The best markets are those combining a horizontal and vertical.

An example of a vertical market is plumbers. Other examples are teachers, authors, actors, it doesn't matter.

Now apply the horizontal model on top of that, 'wanting to make money.' You're finding groups within these groups that are more likely to need your product. The horizontal market is wide, it crosses all sorts of verticals.

The same for wellness products.

"Well, everybody wants to be healthy, David."

Oh, come on, "everybody wants to be healthy." That's hardly true.

The world is faced with dire problems due to obesity. Obesity is brought on, except for a very small percentage of people, because of what we do.

We eat too much. No matter what we say, we eat too much.

"But our food today is addictive, full of carbs and sugars, and it's no wonder we get fat."

No one puts a gun to our heads. Don't eat as much, and you lose weight.

FYI: the two biggest groups of yearly best-selling books are cookbooks and diet books. Also, every diet works if you follow it. The reason there are so many new diets is not because the last one didn't work. It's because most people won't stick to it.

That's why there're more and more books on dieting. It's because someone will always believe, "If I just read that book and follow this NEW diet I'll lose weight."

From time to time, when faced with a health scare (our own, or a close friend), a new relationship, or some sort of 'reason,' everyone goes on a 'health kick'. If you are in a wellness MLM you want to market your product to folks who are in that 'health kick' stage. Hit them right then and they are yours.

Health kicks don't last forever and good marketers know that. That's why we keep dripping on them for a while, because sooner or later another 'reason' kicks in. People decide to get 'healthy again' or 'this time I'm going to lose weight' and they may even stick with their MLM.

It's human nature.

I had to learn that and once you embrace it, this business is no longer a mystery.

FYI: You are going to learn in this book to NOT ever say what I have been saying to you now. When you are marketing, you never say to a prospect 'it's your fault.' Never. You will learn that later in this book and you will end up rethinking all you ever thought you knew about marketing and human nature.

When we're marketers, we can't tailor our marketing message to everybody.

The more specific and the more we can tailor our marketing message to somebody, the more likely it is that they'll respond.

If you know your specific target market as well as you know a close friend, you have as much probability of recruiting them into your program.

The more you know about your niche, assuming that you're selling something they need, the better the likelihood you can explain it in such a way they will acquire your products and even join you in the business.

The more you understand your market and can tailor your message, the more success you'll find.

That's the exact opposite of throwing spaghetti against the wall.

Instead, choose a target market or niche and say to yourself, "That's the target market I want and I will learn all about it. I will make my marketing work for those folks and I will specialize in fulfilling their needs, wants, and desires."

You just do that over and over again and you will become increasingly stronger in that particular niche. Then you'll win big.

This book is about boomers, but targeting works for teachers, mortgage brokers, real estate agents, soccer moms, single moms, stay at home dads, and crafters. It doesn't matter.

Once you get started on a particular niche or a vertical market and you get good at talking their language, you will win.

Additionally, on the subject of language, I always recommend that you can find a market you're familiar with or even a part of.

This is because you know their lingo, their jargon, and their frame of reference. We're going to be talking about this in the case of boomers, including their hopes, dreams, and desires.

Knowing these things will get you walking across the stage.

It's one of the reasons I've become a good marketer. I studied human nature. Just by being in network marketing, I became self-taught and learned how to focus a concept that I later learned was called empathy.

Empathy essentially puts you in the shoes of the other person or niche. NOT to sympathize with them but to empathize with them. That means understanding their needs, wants, and desires. Once you can do that, you'll know what they need and can tailor your message to help them get what they need.

If you don't have something that they need, don't bother trying to sell it to them.

Some people say 'I'll talk to anyone.' This practice is hurting our industry. It makes us look like cultists.

Our job is not to 'spread the Word,' it is to let interested parties know we have something that already interests them. They just don't know our particular product or business, yet.

FYI there are people who even say in their testimonials, 'I wasn't looking for the business. It found me.' These folks are wrong. They just have not realized there was something missing in their lives that our business fulfills. You can't put more than 1 quart of water in a 1-quart jug).

For example, I deal with a lot of people in the anti-aging business. There're a lot of people who say to me, "Yes, the 20-somethings are now interested in keeping their looks and they are spending money on anti-aging products. I'm going to go after that market."

Really. Really?

Why? It's the least likely market.

Remember our discussion about probabilities.

Sure, some of those in their twenties are spending money on anti-aging products. Compare this to people who are older and have a much stronger desire to look younger:

Do I have to say it?

Don't be dumb.

The trend is your friend.

Casinos make money because of probabilities.

You can bet on that.

There's a saying in the insurance industry that it's a lot easier to sell insurance when the hearse is in the driveway.

When we see death on the doorstep, we want insurance.

Sell to people who see the need. Whatever market you pick, choose one with a need for your product.

When selling your opportunity, only speak with those in the 20% club. Forget nine-to-fivers.

Clearly we're going to focus on boomers in this book, but the lesson is to learn about your niche and bring them what they care about. It is not what you care about or what your upline cares about. It isn't even what your company president cares about.

You'll find your riches in niches.

You can pick another niche too. Once you have mastered one, pick another one. Then, pick another one. As long as you apply the same formula to all markets find out their needs, wants and desires, secret dreams and ambitions. If you do that, you will be successful.

That's the concept behind niche marketing. It's better than throwing spaghetti against the wall.

It's better than buying leads.

When you buy leads, for example, that's just a big horizontal market. It's very wide. Everybody wants to make money taking a survey online.

So, the list you buy is full of disjointed greedy people who clicked some cheesy ad offering riches.

Have you noticed that these types of prospects are hard to find? Perhaps you noticed they can be hard to follow up on and hard to reach because it's such a common denominator?

They all think, "Yeah, I need more money." You didn't get a group of leads that are willing to do something about it beyond click they make.

That's why I hate online leads. Most of them are crap and to get anything out of the very expensive ones, you've got to be a telephone solicitor in order to engage them.

That's okay if that's what you're into. But I prefer going after a very specific and targeted niche. Going after a very narrow niche, like dentists, doctors, chiropractors, teachers, soccer moms, body-builders, holistic workers, small business owners, day-traders, to name a few, will make your job easier.

Boomers are a wide niche, but are still easy to target once you apply some filters to weed out the 80% who are not worth our time.

If you learn about any niche that makes sense to use as your target market, you can be successful in this business.

We're going to cover boomers in this book but just so you know, in the next chapter we're going to talk about how to understand the needs, wants, and desires of your target niche. In this next chapter, I will teach you how to understand any niche you wish.

Getting Inside the Head of Your Target Market so you can craft the Perfect Pitch

This chapter is very important, and while we're going to be 'getting in the heads' of Boomers, we're also going to do so with another group called network marketers.

That will help you get the idea of how this process works.

My method of getting into the head of my niche has changed over the years. You have the advantage of learning this from me today and not years ago.

One person who really helped me fine-tune this is Dan Kennedy, who I recommend you study if you want to learn direct marketing. However, his trainings are very expensive and more complex than we need for networking.

I just wanted you to have his name in case you want to get more in-depth on this.

The way to do it is to play a question – answer game with yourself where you take the role of your target market. You need to be able to answer these questions and if you can't, you need to research the answers. I chose to use networkers as the target for this chapter because you know networkers and you are one. As such, you should be able to answer these questions or at least see how the answers fit for our group.

Question 1: What keeps your target market or your prospect awake at night?

Now, if we're talking about network marketers, ask yourself, 'what keeps a network marketer awake at night?'

When I first got involved in the industry, I sponsored some people I knew. I remember sitting bolt upright in bed, after midnight, only two weeks into the program, before I even made a check.

I couldn't sleep and I kept saying to myself, "My gosh, what if people whom I get involved in this don't succeed? What if I don't succeed? They'll all point their finger at me and say,

'Thanks for getting me involved in this, you didn't even make any money.'"

That night I just made a decision: "I am going to succeed."

It was the only way I could get back to sleep.

Making that commitment helped me.

That lack of 100% commitment keeps a lot of networkers up at night.

I'm sure there're a lot of people who get involved in this industry who are presently worrying about whether they're going to succeed. Not just because of their own selfish interests, such as their bank account, but for the fact that they have involved other people.

They are afraid that these folks are going to point the finger at them. "Well Bob, David, Mary, and whomever, you didn't succeed either, so you want to buy that stuff back from me?"

That is a fear. It can stop people from going to their warm market.

Often we think folks won't go to their warm market because they are afraid of getting the 'No' answer, but mostly it's because they are afraid of getting a yes when they, themselves, are not 100% committed.

That's right. It's not the fear of rejection. Sometimes it's the fear of believing we're responsible for other people's success.

Once we are committed, we don't fear our warm market. If our warm market says no, the 100% committed person does not care.

If they say 'yes,' the 100% committed person doesn't take responsibility for their success because they know no one else can take responsibly for anyone else's success.

People will succeed with or without you.

But for those with a lack of 100% commitment, there is a fear. You need to understand all these fears when you market to your niche.

FYI, if you have any of those fears, read my Mindset book because a DMO acted upon is the only cure for that fear. Seen end of the book for information on my Mindset book and other resources.

Now that we are getting the idea, let's ask ourselves what else keeps a networker up at night?

I know people are constantly wondering, "Where am I going to find people?"

That dreaded word 'L E A D S.'

That's one of the reasons you're reading this book. It's because you're interested in Boomers as a group to market to.

Maybe you're one of those people who is worrying, "I know the industry. I love my product. I love my company. I love the concept, but I don't know who to talk to."

I will wager that most people who give you a negative answer about network marketing are in the same boat. They are negative because they don't think they can find anyone to talk to.

If you don't believe me, try this thought experiment: What would a prospect do if you were able to guarantee that you have 100 people just waiting to join up as soon as they are asked?

Suddenly all the phony excuses evaporate and they'll get started.

If you can find a way to target a market successfully, then you can overcome objections like 'I don't know anyone. Where do I find people?'

For example, I know when I talk to people to whom I had sent a postcard and answered, love the idea of using postcards.

That's why people mostly ask you, 'How did you get my name?'

I speak to them about postcard marketing so I can eliminate the fear of 'how do I find people' before I even tell them about the company, products, etc....

No matter what product you offer, those people who have tried networking in the past are very interested if you can show them a way that they can find people with an easy approach.

That is so much more important than how old your company is. Company age is vastly over-rated.

All prospects are wondering "Where do I find people?"

It's a big frustration and it will keep people awake at night.

Another frustration for network marketers is the thought they will sponsor people, followed by more people, and then more people but they might not do anything. That idea keeps networkers awake at night.

They have 80 people in their group, hit a good level or rank, and yet they are not making the kind of money all the examples seem to show.

They begin to wonder if it's all a lie.

FYI this is not a book about recruiting networkers, but if you are in this position, you must learn this hard reality. "It's not the numbers in your organization, it's the organization in your numbers."

We're not here to answer all the worries of our industry, but it's an exercise you should be able to do yourself. Write down all the things that either frustrates your niche or that which keeps your niche awake at night.

Another one for networkers is, "Nobody takes me seriously." and "I never made ten thousand dollars so why should people listen to me?"

FYI, using my Branding book will help you through this problem!

If you know and really understand what it is that is causing your target market to stay awake at night, you can find a way to help them. If you can't find a way to help them, then you can cross that worry off your list. At least you understand your market better and that's really important.

Question 2: Whom does your niche market or prospect blame for their problems?

In this next step start assessing everything from the first question and ask yourself, "Well, who do they blame for all the things that go wrong?"

Who do they think caused their problems? Who is responsible for their problems?

Using our network marketing example, "Who does the network marketer blame if he or she isn't succeeding?"

Now here, you need to know a little bit about psychology. Just a little bit will help. This is important. Most of us, I would say all of us, don't want to blame ourselves even when we make mistakes. We do something wrong or we don't do what we should be doing. When we don't work hard, or work hard but NOT on what we really should be doing, we don't want to blame ourselves when things naturally don't pan out.

We'll give ourselves an out. We want to blame somebody else. To blame somebody else is human nature.

You've heard of a scapegoat. The scapegoat excuse is part of human nature.

You're never going to be successful by saying to somebody, "It's your fault and it's your mistake."

If you are training a group you can get away with it, but don't do it in your marketing or PR.

I love to listen to Jim Rohn and send people to take his recorded trainings. Nearly all personal development is to take responsibility for our actions, life, and future.

That's all well and good, but NEVER ever in your marketing. No one wants to have their nose rubbed in it.

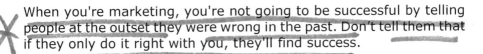

When you're marketing, you're not going to be successful by telling people at the outset they were wrong in the past. Don't tell them that if they only do it right with you, they'll find success.

You can't do that. If you do that, they'll just say "no" because you've just told them that they're the problem.

Think about your own relationship. How does your partner react when you tell them they are the reason for their problems?

Now, going back to our list of problems. It's what people think is the cause of the problems, but is not the real cause. It's the person in the mirror.

The question is who they might blame?

And, by the way, I'm not saying this is right or wrong. Marketing is basic psychology. Who does your prospect blame for their woes?

Often networkers will blame an upline or the guy or girl that got them into the business. They'll blame anyone but themselves.

Boomers, for example, may blame the government or the greedy bankers for the economic slow-down. Excuses may include, "I lived in the wrong city and all the industry moved out," or

"My parents told me to get a job learning how to make vinyl records, and then the industry died." It's always somebody else's fault, but you need to know who the perceived enemy is.

If I'm recruiting network marketers, there's plenty of people that they'll blame. They'll blame lead generators or the people that recommend them.

Personally, I don't like online lead generators and lead sellers because the leads are usually crap, but nobody has to buy them.

You can't say it's the fault of the buyer. If you do, you just made an enemy!

The bottom line is this: You want to know who they blame.

For Boomers it's often Obama, or Bush. It doesn't matter. And one administration always blames the last.

During the Clinton administration, there was the phrase 'It's the economy, stupid.' This meant it's not the current leadership who's to blame. It's the economy.

You need to know who your niche blames for their ills because, in your marketing, you need to be able to set up that enemy.

You need to be able to show that you are going to be able to eliminate their enemy for them to be successful.

Or the power of that enemy.

If greedy bankers caused the economic disaster (as far as your niche is concerned), then your message may be one of those videos we see that start off like this:

"Were you one of the victims of the 2008 recession? Lost your job to China? Found out your pension is not even something you can live on? Well, ..."

Karatbars (Gold MLM) does a lot of this very well.

Look, we're not talking about manipulating people, here. Lots of this is true.

To look at it a different way, would you think marketing should sound like this?

"Did you know the economy goes in cycles, watched the loaning of money to those with poor credit ratings, saw banks buy junk debt, and still thought it would last forever? Were you someone who thought the laws of economics were magic, and not real? Well, time to get with it and get to work. Starvation is your future if you don't get off your lazy butt. Call me now and I'll tell you more reasons you were so stupid and why you need someone like me to tell you what to do. By the way, have your credit card ready."

In a way, we do manipulate people. However, because we join companies we believe in, with products we actually use, I believe networking is far more honorable than other industries.

We're not selling people swampland in Florida. We're talking about selling people a really good opportunity we have also bought into and believe in.

We need to be able to speak on our niche's level and understand that there is a perceived enemy. As a marketer, that's the enemy you must show you can slay.

FYI: In the Cold War, we all had an enemy. It was the Soviet Union. Later, we found out that enemy was not as strong as we thought. The CIA was kind of lost afterward because they didn't have an enemy anymore. Without getting into history, you understand that having an enemy, whether real or imagined, is part of human nature. Understand who your target market believes to be the enemy.

Question 3: What major frustrations does your niche have? Are these different from the frustrations they face on a daily basis?

For network marketers, it can be finding someone to talk to. It can be that we feel we are not being taken seriously. It can be that the people we were following up on seem to never be available because they don't answer the phone or emails, and have potentially entered the witness protection program.

Sometimes, it's the negativity in the newspapers about our industry, company, or even our product.

Phosphates really made our laundry clean and for many years Amway used it. Once it was banned Amway was in the press and it meant Amway representatives had to deal with jokes and negativity.

Today, Herbalife is under attack by some fat cats on Wall St. Don't think it can't happen to your company or product.

Within our industry, wellness companies compete with each other by simply adding something 'more' to their product than you have in yours.

I call these 'me too' products. When one product is doing well, other companies are forced to offer 'me too' products to compete.

These are just part of the frustrations that we networkers go through.

In most cases, your experienced upline can deal with it. I can shoot holes in any of these frustrations, but that's because I've got years under my belt and know to defeat the 'fear factor.' I can stop people from chasing after the next bright shiny object.

The key is this: you need to know what frustrations your target market has. Whether they are network marketers or Boomers, you need to be able to understand them.

Question 4: What does your niche secretly desire?

You are not just interested in the little things. What do they secretly desire most? What is their hidden fantasy?

This is really important.

Using our network marketer example, know that the answer to their secret desire is not having an unlimited lead supply. It can't be secret desire if it's not a secret!

What does the distributor sitting in the audience at their company's convention secretly want the most?

They want to be called to the stage.

They want to be praised for success.

They want to have 20,000 people cheering for them!

With their family in the audience and their team numbering in the thousands, the network marketer secretly desires to see them all smiling, cheering, and giving them a standing ovation.

This is an example of a secret fantasy for all networkers.

Another examples is the secret desire to have the ability to buy a brand new luxury car. It can be the desire to drive over to a friend's house and show it off. Especially if it is a friend that didn't want to join the network when things first got started. The fantasy may even include a dialogue:

"Oh, you got a new car! It's beautiful. But where can you park it?"

"Well, we're moving to a new 8 bedroom estate."

"Really? How can you afford it?"

"You know, that company I got involved in. Remember, the one you laughed at?"

"Really? Oh my gosh, I should have listened to you."

A secret fantasy is that they want their parents, husband or wife, and others they care about, to stop saying, "Why don't you get a real job?" Network marketers would rather hear, "It's great what you've done. I'm really proud of you, my dear. I'm really proud of you, son. You've really come a long way."

A secret fantasy for network marketers is to have lunch with the ladies who snickered behind their back because they were 'selling'.

"She sells makeup. Are you still selling makeup, Mary?"

"Well, yes."

"Oh that's nice for you. How many customers do you have? I guess you have all your friends, so about 3 or 4?"

"Oh, about 22,482 customers in 5 continents, in 33 countries."

"What?!!!!!!!!!"

These are the secret desires of people in our industry.

When you know this, it becomes easy to stop saying things like, "Hey, you could make more money." You'll find you can replace those words and instead, paint word pictures for people about their hopes and dreams.

I'm sure there isn't a reader who hasn't thought about and day-dreamed things like this. We all do, if we're being honest with our-selves.

If you have these same dreams and secret fantasies, learn to recognize and understand the same is true for your niche. You'll be able to get into the mind of your market and match your marketing so make a true connection.

In the next few chapters, we're going to talk about Boomers and their thoughts, desires, and dreams. In the last chapters, we're going to talk about how can use those particular emotions to market.

You know what's really great about Boomers?

The fact that so many network marketers today are Boomers, them-selves!

Underlying Psychological Factors You Need to Know to Market to Boomers successfully

Psychological Factor 1: Longevity Matters to Boomers

Why?

Simple – They have been around longer than anybody else. Of course, this applies to seniors too. For boomers, if you tell them that your company is 18 years old this is not a negative.

To them, it is a positive statement, and this is important because a lot of people in marketing will promote that companies are brand-new or still gaining momentum.

If you are dealing with a boomer experienced in network marketing, don't just make a big deal that your company is brand new. They, more than most, know the importance of experience, especially on their management team.

To a boomer, a solid older company is probably going to be around for another 20 years.

FYI: A millennial doesn't care about this as much. In fact, an older company may seem like a negative to them, but for a boomer it makes a difference.

So, what do you say if you are promoting a brand new company to a boomer?

Meaning, how do you paint the picture to a boomer to give them confidence in something new and unproven?

An example would be to say, "While the company is brand new, the management team has been in this industry for over 20 years, and we have a combined industry experience of over 80 years."

Another example may be the development of your product. Perhaps it has taken many years of research and development. If there were some scientists who had been on this for over 20 years before the company bought the rights to the product, talk about that lengthy commitment to 20 years of scientific research. Include the fact that while the company is new, the science is established, proven, and tested.

Examples of positive and negative words:

If you want to sound positive about 'age' or longevity, don't comment that it is an old company. Instead, say it's an experienced company. The same goes when you are dealing with boomers. You don't want to say somebody is old. You want to say somebody is experienced.

Psychological Factor 2: Authority and Credibility Matter to Boomers

Now that you are thinking along the lines of longevity and why it matters you can understand the second psychological factor. Authority and credibility are very important factors for boomers.

Again, due to having had a longer life, authority and credibility are much more important to a boomer than a millennial.

A millennial, as we discussed, doesn't care that much about how long a company has been in business. A new company is much more fashionable.

They also don't care as much about authority. They look more for celebrity status, and this is less so with boomers. However, boomers have their celebrities, but authorities count for more.

Doctors have great authority status to boomers.

Doctors, authors, experts, people like Oprah, and people like Dr. Oz. If your product is in some way positively identified by a doctor or well-known celebrity, which has authority, then this situation is very positive and good to promote.

For example, if you are allowed to mention how Dr. Oz or Oprah spoke highly of your product's main ingredient.

If you can say 'as seen on TV' or 'as mentioned in the NY Times' this authority looks very good to Boomers.

On the subject of doctors, nearly every large network marketing company has doctors involved in some way. They may be on the board the company is in the wellness industry. Even if you are not a wellness company, there are generally, a lot of doctors involved in network marketing.

Because boomers pay such close attention to the authority you should keep track of testimonials given by doctors for your product.   It doesn't matter if your product has nothing to do with health.

To a boomer, a doctor is a doctor. To see this in action, see my book on Recruiting Doctors.

If a doctor says Amway products are good, or Legal Shield is a great company, this carries weight for boomers. It's an important endorsement.

For millennials, it is different. It doesn't trigger that much meaning for them.

Boomers also accept advice from authority figures. If you have read my book on branding and are putting it to use, then you can state that you are an expert, and you can market yourself as one online. With this, you are going to have much more credibility with a boomer.

Sometimes you need to redefine yourself or your company to be recognized as the top in your field. For example, if your company is a number one company in a category and that has become accepted, that's great.

Let's say your company isn't the leader. It is a brand new company, or it is a brand new product, and you don't have any way to claim it is the best at something. In this case, you need to redefine a category or create a new category so you can become a leader.

In other words, if you are not outstanding in your field, find another field. Find a field where you are alone and can now claim leadership.

Let me say this again: you want to be the leader in a category. So, if you are not the leader in someone else's category, create a new category and claim to be the leader there.

You can even do that on a team level.

Let's say you are putting together a team in St. Louis. In this example, you are NOT the largest team in St. Louis. There is another team of distributors from your company that is much older and larger.

You could be the fastest growing team in St. Louis.

Or you could be the only team that does coffee calls four times a week. You could be the only team that has a doctor in the group doing regular presentations.

You need to create something that gives you credibility and authority.

Of course, the way to do that is to find something that's different so you can say you are the leader in that one category.

Fastest growing, as a category, is easy. If you are one person today and two people tomorrow you just doubled in size. That's how you can be fast growing.

It is always easier to be the fastest growing company when you are small rather than large. The smaller group will appear to be faster growing than a larger group when you discuss it in terms of the percentage growth.

Keep that in mind when someone says their company is on the Inc 500.

That's not the only way that you can show positive differentiation. You can also do it with online tools if you create some.

For example, 'Our team has the best and most advanced video presentations'.

Networkers have been doing this for years, but this is really important to boomers, as long as you can explain to them what it means. If you are speaking a language they don't understand, it won't make any sense.

Fortunately, most boomers have had some experience in network marketing because of their age. It's much more refreshing than having to train somebody without experience. So, if they do understand what you are talking about its fine to use jargon but DON'T use jargon if it is not universal.

People don't like to look stupid so they won't ask you what a word means.

Here is another example of the difference between millennials and boomers in regards to authority, credibility, and longevity.

The term 'virtual corporation' is a negative term to a boomer.

Let me explain.

If a millennial says to his parents, "Yeah, I am using a new type of bank. It's a virtual bank with no offices. It just has ATMs and an online presence."

His boomer parents will ask, "Well, son where are they located?"

"Oh, it is a virtual bank. It is all over the internet. They don't actually have branch offices".

To a boomer, this is ridiculous. They understand the term 'virtual' to mean 'nearly real, but not real.'

To a millennial a virtual corporation means it is everywhere. It is omnipresent.

So, the same word, virtual, has very different meanings depending on who hears it.

You need to understand the language when you are dealing with boomers and how they assess the meanings of words. The word 'virtual' is not a strong thing.

They grew up with authority and solid brick and mortar businesses. 'Give me something I can sink my teeth into' 'hands on experience' and 'a solid foundation.' These are strong tactile word messages to boomers.

There are reasons for why boomers follow authority.

When boomers were growing up if their parents asked them to do something and they questioned why, the answer was 'because I said so.'

Today young people don't buy that concept.

In the good old days, police were honest, and you listened to the police. Authority figures were strong.

For example Presidents like Reagan were considered strong. If the president wasn't strong, he didn't last more than four years (i.e., Jimmy Carter, Ford). Even Clinton was a positive president because he was considered strong by boomers. The same is true with former President Bush.

Typically boomers tend to be conservative. They may have liberal attitudes, but they tend to be conservative with their money. Of course, some of them are conservative politically as well. This is neither good nor bad. It is just the way it is.

Lastly, on the subject of authority and credibility, we'll talk about authorship.

Boomers put a great value on authorship. I am going to be putting together a product that will help you get a book published, a physical book.

eBooks are okay, but for boomers, an eBook is like a virtual book. There is very little value.

If you can show a boomer a physical book, they value it, and therefore they value the author.

What if you are not an author? Create copy from real books that suggest your product's main ingredient is great and add that to your presentation.

If you have a non-physical product, like energy, there are a many great quotes and financial articles about the market for energy.

FYI: a physical book is the best business card you can ever have.

Psychological Factor 3: Attention Span

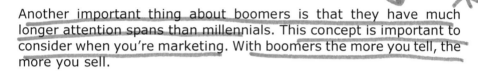

Another important thing about boomers is that they have much longer attention spans than millennials. This concept is important to consider when you're marketing. With boomers the more you tell, the more you sell.

You will still hear people shouting about the need to have shorter and shorter videos and shorter presentations. Yes, to a degree but not to the degree that the millennials will want.

If your presentations require long meetings or webinars, the millennial will be looking at their smartphone and will become bored more quickly than the boomer.

Boomers have a longer attention span, and they also like physical media like hard copy books and materials you can hold and feel.

I am going to cover more of this in the later chapters, but boomers are more likely watch a physical DVD if you mail them one than a millennial.

There is also a greater likelihood a boomer will watch it whether it is half an hour or even an hour long as long as it is interesting.

Hey, if something is not interesting you are not going to get anyone to watch it!

Psychological Factor 4: Guilt

Boomers have been brought up with guilt. Their parents often motivated them by withdrawing love or making them feel guilty for what they did.

Today we know this is NOT the way to bring up a child, but 60 years ago it was the norm. It is crushing to a child, but no one knew any better.

You can motivate people this way too. For example, I was coaching a lady who did a great job presenting her product to a prospect, a boomer mother.

The product was Juice Plus, which is essentially enzymes.

The boomer she was selling to was, in fact, the grandmother who was raising two grandchildren. The mother wasn't in the picture, so the boomer grandmother was raising two children as if she was the mother.

The lady I was coaching did a great job 'selling' to the boomer grandmother the importance of Juice Plus, which I think was $60-70 per month.

The prospect said no because she would feel guilty taking it. She was convinced her grandchildren, daughter and husband should also take it, and she could not afford it for all of them.

The person I was coaching asked me, "How do I sell this product so she does not feel guilty being the only one taking it?"

I said we need to motivate the person the same way - with guilt.

This example is just like the airlines. When you are about to take off, and they are doing the safety presentation, they always talk about the cabin pressure decreasing, which will cause oxygen masks to drop from the ceiling. Then they instruct us to put our oxygen mask on first, and then help children put on their mask.

At face value, it sounds terrible. It is almost reflex to think it should be children first.

Airlines tell us this because your child is going to panic, and will fight you while you are trying to put on their mask. You could both die, whereas if you put yours on first, then you will be breathing fine and can take the time you need to put the mask on your child.

You don't want your child to die, right? That's guilt.

It is the same thing with Juice Plus.

"Your kids are actually fine without taking these enzymes right now. At this age, even though we have a product for the children, you are the one who is primarily responsible for your family's well-being. You are cooking for your husband, cleaning for your family, cooking for the kids, bringing them up, and raising them. If something happened to your health, you are the linchpin here. They are all going to suffer. You'd feel pretty bad if you didn't protect your health and ended up letting your family down, wouldn't you?'

I feel guilty even telling you that story!

Why the 'Working Smart Pitch' is NOT Smart

One of the great things about Boomers is the fact that they learned to be optimistic.

They were competitive. Workaholics were not a bad thing, and they liked having visible success. If you think back in the 80s when, if you are a Boomer, everybody was driving BMWs, dressed in double-breasted power suits.

If you went to a network marketing meeting in the 80s and early 90s, that's how people dressed because of the age group.

The movie Wall Street said greed was good; it was a prime champion of people who were success motivated. Now, certainly not everybody was in that frame of mind, but in the times when things were going well, there were a lot of fond memories from that period.

Greed was not a negative word. It meant you did not mess around or leave money on the table.

For example, if you ask boomers, Ronald Reagan is still considered one of the top presidents in the United States. So hard work was not considered a bad word with boomers. Sometimes this is a big challenge with networkers.

"You don't need to work hard."

"Hard work is for schmucks."

"Work smart, not hard."

"Four hour work week"

Phrases like this are taken to be suspicious by boomers. If you ask them what it means, they'll reply, "It means Scam."

Unless you can articulate what working smart means and show exactly why hard work is bad, you can show up looking a huckster. Boomers don't see hard work as a negative. They see hard work as something you have to do to have some success.

If you have a very good income or you're talking about somebody who has a very good income in terms of your business, and you say, "Oh, it's easy. It's simple. You don't have to work hard. We do all the heavy lifting for you." These expressions don't make sense to boomers.

If it doesn't make sense - it's got to be a scam.

Now it doesn't mean you need to lead with phrasing about how difficult it will be, but you want your marketing to make sense.

Let's face it, making 10K per month is hard work.

I think the best way to describe your business is to say you have a small part-time income for people who are looking for just that. We have a mid-sized income for people who are willing to put in 20 hours a week. We also have people earning 10, 20, 30 thousand dollars a month - but they are willing to work really hard. For those looking to go in that direction, it's possible if they work for it.

When you say it and express it like that, it makes sense.

Bottom line: If you're dealing with Boomers, be up front about the work and explain it: let the boomer make their choice.

What is the right Frame of Reference?

The next thing you need to think about in terms of boomers is their frame of reference.

Boomers remember back to their very first real purchase. Their first major investment in a real estate deal, how much did that house cost? This can vary depending on where they lived in the country, but that's how they remember prices.

Most of us remember our first car, and the price of gasoline when we first had to pay for it on our own.

So when boomers look at the cost of something, they relate it back to the first purchase of its kind, or something similar.

You probably got tired of your parents saying, "Well when I was your age, milk was only ten cents and movies only cost five cents."

It's not a negative. It's not a positive. It's just a fact of life. So when you go and express the cost to join your program along with a product purchase you need to consider this.

Let's say, for example, its $1000, $500, $2000, whatever. Don't be surprised that you get a reaction of negativity that that's a lot of money.

Boomers remember when $2000 was a down payment on their first home, and now they are looking at your 12 jars of product X for $1000?

So you need to do a fantastic job explaining value over price.

As another example, cosmetics used to cost only x amount of money. Also, vitamins used to cost only x. They don't go to stores buying expensive vitamins. It's great if you have people who are used to that, but that's not always going to happen.

Today there are very few things less expensive than they used to be. Computers and televisions used to be very expensive, and today in comparison are very inexpensive. If you talk to millennials, and you speak about spending $1000 on a laptop, they see that is a lot of money. Apps are just a few bucks.

I look back, and I remember routinely spending between $3000 to $5000 for a laptop or desktop, and that was when there was no Internet. Computers didn't offer as much value as they do today.

Each age group has a different frame of reference for things.

A millennial may see $600 for a phone as reasonable, whereas boomers just shake their heads.

"You paid $600 for a smartphone? Are you confused, son?" says the boomer.

In my opinion phones have been marketed poorly to boomers, because they use the word, 'phone'. Call it a computer that acts as a phone that you can carry around and the boomer will say, "Oh yeah, a computer."

That makes sense to them because it's a powerful computer that fits in your pocket, and it can communicate like a phone. Skype with grandkids, read books, play bridge, get directions, keep track of your meds and health. It's much more than a phone.

In any event, it's millennials who buy the smartphones while you'll still see a lot of boomers using desktops and laptops.

So, how do you deal with the price when discussing a product with a boomer?

You deal with the price the same way when anybody says something is expensive.

First, you have to acknowledge the price to yourself. It's not that you're admitting it's expensive, but you have to acknowledge it to figure out a solution.

I like to use this equation: Value equals Price.

You need to be able to change it to: Value exceeds Price.

You need to express your pitch, so the value is increased. You do not, using our example, allow your boomer prospect to see your offer of a startup purchase as 12 bottles of skincare for $1000. You need to explain the value of one of those bottles as equivalent to, for example, 32 treatments at a spa. And each spa treatment is $60 per visit. So it's 32 times $60, which is $1920 dollars of Value in each jar!

Now just include the intrinsic value, "What is it worth to you to look younger if you're in the job market? What is it worth to you to get that job promotion because you look better?"

You need to keep layering value over price over and over until the value is so much bigger, it no longer equals the price. The value must be huge compared to the price.

If you've ever watched any internet marketing presentations, and I'm sure you have, you'll see this concept at the end of the presentation, or as we call it in sales, "the close."

It's classic.

For example, you will hear the presenter say, "Okay, you want to know what the price is. Before I tell you the price, let me tell you the value of this. If you are going to go and build this software yourself, and you had to hire programmers it would cost you $5000. Now let me tell you what the bonuses are going to be today. A, B, and C. Each one of these bonuses are worth $2000. So the total value is $11,000."

"Now you're not going to pay $11,000. You're not going to pay $5000. You're not going to pay $1000. You're only going to pay $299."

Wow, you're in!

So what they've done is exactly what I've briefly shown you. They have increased the value over the price.

By stating the so-called value in terms of the boomer doing creating the product or working on this themselves. The DIY pitch, if you will.

Of course, they do this in a longer format. But this is what you need to be able to do for your product. You need to be able to do that verbally; you need to be able to do that in print. You need to be able to do that in your emails and your closing, and you need to do this in a meeting.

Don't tell somebody it's $1000, and then wait for them to say it's too expensive for them. If you do this properly in your marketing, when the person sees the price for your 12 jars of skin care cream for $1000, they see it as only $1000.

"Oh, boy, I thought you were going to tell me it would be $10,000!"

"Dissing" and Respect

Boomers feel that they deserve respect. They have worked very hard, often still work, and will likely work for a very long time. Some of them lost a lot of money. Some lost all their money in 2008.

But no matter what, they feel they deserve something from this country, from society, from you, from millennials, from everybody for what they've done to help build the opportunities that are now available in this country.

Now everybody feels that they deserve respect. But boomers feel they deserve respect because of what they've done and what they have gone through. If you are younger and are ignoring that sense of earned respect, and you're aiming at the boomer market, you are in trouble.

Emotion

Another difference between boomers and millennials is the fact that boomers don't display all their emotions on their sleeve.

Boomers don't share all their financial frustrations nor all their emotional problems on Facebook.

When boomers read stories about 20-somethings writing on their Facebook page about getting drunk, being hungover at their 'crappy job,' and then feeling shocked about getting fired over it, boomers just shake their heads and laugh.

They don't shake their head because they don't understand, they shake their head at the stupidity of it. They were brought up in a time when you keep stupid things to yourself.

For boomers, you don't air your dirty laundry. Boomers were brought up not to gossip about other people. And they would never even think about gossiping about themselves to the world!

To them, what millennials post or show on Facebook is ridiculous. They are concerned about the things people say and send over Twitter, including people who post nearly naked pictures.

Boomers keep their emotions in check.

If you look at the different versions of Star Trek, consider the very first original series. It was very gutsy with lots of fighting and action. The men were proud, and the woman wore short skirts. That was the era of the 60s. James Tiberius Kirk was always fighting and womanizing. He didn't cry or teach yoga.

When Star Trek the Next Generation found its way on to the set it was very different. People were more emotional and empathic and cared about what other people thought.

This is like that younger generation of today. So I'm not referring to which is the better Star Trek, I'm referring to the viewer mindset.

If you want to market to boomers, don't expect them to open up to you like a millennial will.

It's a sign of disrespect to say as whether a boomer is broke or having a hard time paying their bills?

You can speak about it to a group, but don't push it one-on-one, unless you are dealing with a warm market.

If you purchase a list of people who are having a hard time paying the bills, then you can make that assumption. You don't need to ask. If they respond to an ad that's in that direction, make that assumption. Don't push them and ask.

Here's an advantage for this lack of emotional openness among Boomers. If you're offering a network marketing option and suggest a $1000 product purchase, and your boomer prospect doesn't have a $1000, they'll often go and find it.

They may tell you that they don't have it, and that's fine. If they want to share their situation with you, great. It means you've shown some respect for them and they trust you.

If they appear to stall you it may just mean they are hitting their connections and trying to find the money.

Of course, generally speaking, if someone tells you right up front, "Hey, I'm broke. Everybody I know is broke. I don't have any money." That's not a good prospect.

If you're marketing to boomers, they either have the money or they have more opportunities for finding it than a millennial.

To sum it up, your frame of reference should be in terms of price. Build that into your close if you have something perceived as expensive for a boomer. Make sure you build in the value ahead of your close.

Give respect to boomers. This is a great way of communicating with boomers because they're not getting any respect from the job market.

It's expensive to hire a boomer because right now a company must pay a much higher cost for health benefits, so it's cheaper to hire a millennial.

But the boomers have the experience. If you say to a boomer, "Listen, we've got something where you can use your experience." That's going to get their attention.

Lastly, pay respect to them for all those years of hard work. Then understand and admire their privacy. Understand and connect with them regarding their willingness to not share everything with strangers on the Internet. If you are not a boomer, don't share your drunken stories with them – you won't get any respect!

Marketing Methods to Prospect Boomers – not your everyday Facebook Ad

What you need to know about boomers and technology. It's not what you would expect

We discussed the different groups of boomers, but you can also divide boomers into tech savvy and non-tech savvy.

One of the challenges of networking marketing is assuming everybody is like ourselves. We assume they are very excited about the business. If we happen to be tech savvy, we assume everybody else is tech savvy or at least has the level of expertise we have.

Many boomers I know are extremely tech savvy. I don't even know if I would call myself tech-savvy. I don't know how to design and create an app, but I know how to find out if that is even something that I would want to do or learn. So, I would consider myself savvy enough to be able to figure things out, yet I don't think that is something that is true for everybody.

For example, I have a dislike of WordPress, yet it's routinely proven to be simple and was designed to be that way. On the other hand, I know how to outsource what I don't know, or what I want to learn about WordPress.

One of the challenges we have to deal with are boomer prospects who are not network marketers and who haven't sat behind a computer for a long time. Most likely if they do sit behind a computer, it's to send emails to grandchildren and do minor surfing.

In fact, a major study was done on boomers for a financial products company, by an interesting fellow named Matt Zagula. What he found was fascinating, and I think this is so important for us to understand.

First of all, 34% of this group bought or purchased financial products or services due to word-of-mouth, which is what we call warm market or warm market referral.

Also, 33% made purchase decisions because of offers from direct mail, educational seminars, and workshops. Direct mail can be postcards, letters or lumpy mail, and of course 'educational seminars and workshops are just 'opportunity meetings' with the added element of good information. This concept is something that is for networkers to adopt.

Another 15% came from television, radio, and newspaper advertising. This statistic is something networkers with co-op advertising can do too.

Social Media, zero.

I want to repeat that. Social Media, zero.

Now, I know that some of you get leads and business from social media. I know networkers that do, but you want to be sure it's working for you. If you find you are wasting your time on social media, go back to what works. Just be aware, you may not find a lot of boomers on social media if that is your aim.

FYI: Prospecting via social media requires serious dedication and long-term vision. It's about developing relationships first and doing sales with the 'oh by the way' approach. You still need a sales funnel through which to run your prospect.

This study applies to somewhat affluent boomers who are purchasing financial products, which is a great market. It is a market that is constantly ignored by networkers because they feel that people with money don't need more money.

This is 'stinkin thinkin,' as Zig would say.

This ignored market is why many people are reluctant to talk to doctors and dentists and lawyers and what you have. If you look at the network marketing success magazines and the testimonials of the top performers, many come from these professional backgrounds. Somehow we routinely see networkers go out there and recruit from the bottom, from the people who 'need a business' versus people who may desire joining a different business.

So, if you have reached that point where you're willing to recruit up, and you're looking to prospect in the boomer market then think about these statistics.

First one again, 34% bought due to word of mouth. This statistic is fantastic for our industry. Our industry is all about word of mouth.

FYI – if you are reading this and thinking you don't know any of these folks, so word -of-mouth is not going to work, you are thinking inside the box. Outside the box thinkers enthusiastically say, "Ok, that's fantastic. I found a group that WANTS to spread the word to their warm market. How do I find those people?" Never dismiss a fact you can utilize. Instead, command your subconscious mind to find a way to make use of it.

Once again, when you pursue top quality individuals, those people don't mind talking to their friends who are connected in ways you and I are not. This sub-niche has great connections and likes to use them.

The other great thing about these contacts is even if they have been involved in network marketing before, they aren't the kind to quickly turn their nose down. They are sharp, intelligent people.

Boomers who have money and are connected tend to be intelligent. If you can live a long time and if you have some resources, you have got to have some brains and connections. These kind of people are not going to sneer and look down at network marketing.

Use the Forbes article about how network marketing can be a smart retirement plan. This an excellent article, if you want a copy, send me an email with the word FORBES in it. The lesson is, look for boomers and take advantage of word of mouth referrals. The success rate is phenomenal.

Going back to our study, 33% of prospects came from direct mail offers, and educational seminars and workshops. Let's talk about educational seminars and workshops. That's another word for a meeting, event, or webinar.

We're going to cover those because the way to do presentations today is different from the way we used to do them in the past. I'm going to cover that later in this chapter.

Direct mail. I continue to talk to people about using direct mail. You can purchase or rent a good list because there are a lot of people marketing to boomers for financial services. You can just contact any listing broker and say, "I want, a solid middle-class boomer list." You'll find good quality. It won't be cheap but it will be worthwhile.

NOTE: This is the same with all leads. If you want to have a good quality lead, it costs more money. If you want a bad lead, it's cheap. Bad, low-quality leads don't produce results, and when you get somebody from a bad lead list, they usually don't do anything anyway. Or they may join, but will be the ones calling you back a week later asking, "What have you done for me this week?" Along the same lines, if you give your team bad leads, it's the fastest way for them to quit the business.

Social Media, zero. I have seen people successfully using Facebook and LinkedIn to recruit. Some of the people that get involved are boomers and some are not. It literally means sitting behind the computer all the time contributing help, appearing nice and knowledgeable in discussions, and with EXTREME finesse, setting out breadcrumbs leading people to your sales funnel.

That's not duplicatable. If you were being brutally honest with folks who ask you, "How do you recruit? What do you do?" You would have to say, "I sit at my computer longer than an accountant in tax season."

For me that would be a terrible burden. I wouldn't want to do that.

I am on a computer a lot but I do different things. And one of them is NOT managing my Facebook account. I'm not on Facebook. You do need to really consider if this is something that you want to do and if somebody would be willing to do that. If so, that's fantastic. Bear in mind that in the financial services industry marketing to boomers, zero boomers made purchases through ads they saw on social media.

At the same time, statistics show us boomers are increasingly using online communication to keep in touch with children and grandchildren. This is why they may be getting a Skype account. That's a positive side, but they're not making purchase decisions, which is important.

You can use these tools slowly with boomers. You can ask them whether they will check their email more often, to get on Skype. They don't mind communication, but they are not going jump into your lead generation funnel from a Facebook ad.

If you do want to use Facebook, go after millennials.

Millennials vs. Boomers and Technology

You have to think about the computers and the cameras that computers have these days. Boomers see them as 'Big Brother'. They don't like Big Brother. They were brought up reading the book 1984 by George Orwell, which I recommend you read or at least watch the film version to get the idea, if you're not a boomer. Call it market research.

Invest a couple of hours and read that book. It's an excellent understanding of what boomer mentality is towards the government, computers, cameras and trust.

Millennials see it completely differently. Big Brother to them was just a television show, a reality TV show where everybody got filmed and you got to see what they did and how they thought and who they slept with and who they spoke about behind their back.

As you know, Millennials will post all sorts of negative things about themselves and their family on the net, i.e. on social media, which is just one gigantic database accessible by Big Brother/NSA.

That's the view of a boomer. So, don't put money into social media if you want your ad to attract boomers. Boomers don't see social media as something that they should appreciate. In fact, boomers appreciate privacy where millennials don't. Millennials have a different view of privacy. It remains to be seen whether this will change as they age.

This tells us a lot about trust. If you're going to go after the boomer market don't invest in social media. While boomers may use Facebook, they don't trust it as an advertising source.

Remember, boomers appreciate credibility and authority. If you've written a book or if you're a doctor or if you have some expertise status that will make the difference.

FYI: get my branding book and get yourself branded as an expert, it's very simple to do, and these are the things that boomers appreciate.

Also, remember when we consider the fact that 33% of boomers made buying decisions based on workshops and educational seminars, this is great for us as networkers.

We started in the meeting industry years ago and we continue to do conduct meetings today. A lot of meetings are, no longer in hotels but are smaller meetings in homes.

Another tip you can use from the financial services industry: They have done very well hosting what they call customer appreciation events. All that means is they invite a customer of their product and say, "Look, we're going to have somebody talk about a retirement industry plan. You might find it useful."

They sell it as education, but it's smart marketing too.

That's one thing that we can learn from the Financial Industry about marketing to boomers - providing education in meetings. When you do that and offer some real value, you'll get their attention.

When the financial services industry does this they will give a ticket too, of course. They say, "Hey, this is a customer appreciation event. We're going to have a really important speaker that will deliver an update on the new Pension Reform Bill. Bring somebody who might be interested." It's fairly straightforward, and if you're a boomer of that age, you'll bring somebody.

Fill your meeting with some genuine education that is useful, so it's not seen as a sales pitch.

If you do the same thing I know you will find great success. I know a very successful anti-aging company called Glissandra who does 'Wine and Wrinkles' parties.

Generically we call them PBR's, or private business receptions. Doing this in the home today is an excellent opportunity to bring in people, especially boomers.

This is better than talking about an opportunity meeting.

Tupperware is another example of this. They've done it beautifully. Instead of conducting a meeting or presentation the old fashioned way where you cover a company product compensation plan and testimonials, take a lesson from the financial services industry and the internet marketing industry.

In the Internet Marketing industry, when they're going to sell you something at a high value, they will first give you a free webinar and that webinar will contain actual, useful, actionable information.

Even at the end of that presentation, if you don't purchase something, a good internet marketing webinar will have taught you something. You'll have learned something that you can take away.

That's why people go and listen to them.

If you have product that has some value in and of itself and you can teach people something that they're going to take away whether they purchase it or not you have a winner for boomers. They won't feel scammed.

For example, if you are in the healthcare industry, give them some health care tips. If you are in the energy market, show them how to save energy over and above switching to your company.

Find a way to illustrate a savings to boomers, they love it.

People say to themselves "Oh, that's interesting. I learned something today. I feel I can trust you. I don't mind bringing somebody to this another time because there's a lot of valuable information."

Boomers value education. So, if you can provide it, then you're going to have an excellent explosion in your recruiting activity.

Same thing, for example, in anti-aging. Explain that you educate listeners on the dos and do nots of skin care because of the sun or the ozone layer, or whatever may be most relevant for that age group.

Teach something of value that will apply to anyone who attends whether they sign up or not. They may just come back again, and with a friend.

Here is a sample close if you were in a skin-care opportunity, "You can buy a lot of great skin-care creams to protect your face. L'Oreal has one for $1,000. This company has one for $800. The company that we're affiliated with has one for $299. But whatever you do, go out there and protect your skin if you want to look younger.

"If you would like to have a sample of our product or if you like to purchase it right now, we can arrange that. By the way, we're also interested in people who would like to work with us if you'd like to have a business on the side."

Talk about that because boomers are bored. We'll cover boomer boredom in another part of the book. Boomers are definitely interested in getting into business.

This is the way to do presentations for boomers, and this is one of the key factors you should take away from this book.

If you're looking for the boomer market, give them something of value, and you will win.

If you present live - don't call it a business opportunity meeting. Come up with a clever name that shows value to the person who is attending, whether it's an existing customer or a new prospect.

For example, an educational event or a workshop. Don't hesitate to rent inexpensive venues because you're not expecting huge numbers. You're expecting regular numbers on a regular basis.

Direct Mail

Let's cover snail mail. Boomers pay attention to their mail. If you're with a company that has catalogs or newsletters, these work well with boomers.

If you are a boomer and you've ever taken a cruise, take a look at the massive, expensive, large brochures mailed by the cruise lines. They spend a fortune on printing. Then there's L.L.Bean, J.Crew and all the other catalog companies. Many of the cosmetic makeup companies have mini catalogs. They work with boomers.

They are mailed as part of your prospecting package. Boomers like to order from these catalogs, especially if they can pick up the phone and call an 800 number, rather than be forced to go online. They prefer to pick up the phone and call. If your company can do that it's a tremendous advantage for you.

We will discuss direct mail later in the book.

Direct Mail Magic to Prospect and Recruit Boomers

We've already learned how trust, authority, and credibility are all very important to this group. We know that boomers don't like social media. It ranked last as far as trust is concerned whereas newspapers and magazines rank the highest.

How can we use this in terms of our recruiting, promoting and prospecting?

There's an interesting study by Epsilon on boomers. According to the study, boomers found online blogs the least trustworthy source of information. For this market, don't send them to blogs. Blogs are not going to be something you can make use of.

However, 70% of boomers trust real mail over e-mail. Now it's 50% for the average person but it's 70% for boomers. Half the people that you could be marketing to, whether they're boomers or not, trust real mail more than e-mail, but 70% of boomers trust real mail. That tells you something.

Also, 70% of boomers like getting mail and they sort it the same day. Boomers reported having a heightened emotional response to opening mail. The more tactile, the more heightened that response is. That's what we marketers call 'lumpy mail'.

For example, if you've ever been on a donor list, you may have received a charity sending you a nickel. The headline might say, "This nickel is to demonstrate what it costs to feed a child in Africa."

This tactic works. It's interesting. It's tactile. You can feel the nickel in the envelope and pocket it. It is The Law of Reciprocity. The Law of Reciprocity says people feel obliged to pay it back when they get something free, even if the value is low.

Of course sending the lumpy item must connect with your pitch.

I remember getting a pair of very inexpensive sunglasses once. The headline was interesting. "You're going to need these because after you read this, your bank account is going to be so bright you'll have to be wearing sunglasses."

They were just cheap sunglasses you could buy for a few pennies from China, but it was excellent, lumpy mail.

As long as you can use some connection, lumpy mail is so powerful that people will even send dollar bills and talk about that dollar.

If you Google *Gary Halbert*, and read about some of his exploits in direct mail, you can learn a tremendous amount of what you can do to tie in practically anything. From elastic bands to pennies, even small, inexpensive reprints. These things really do work. Think about using mail. There's a heightened emotional response for boomers when they receive it.

Carrying on with the study, 50% of boomers state privacy is one of the main benefits of real mail over e-mail.

Lastly, only 5% of boomers relied on Facebook. One-third found online either useless or offensive. Remember this statistic before you spend any money on online advertising. It's why we're talking about direct mail.

Coupons.

You've heard of Groupon. Groupon is one of the reasons coupons are growing because people are using them. I realize Groupon is some- thing that is online, but it is something boomers take part in and enjoy. Coupons can be offered through direct mail or online.

Purium, an MLM company positioned in the high-end supplement and superfood niche, has a free $50 gift card.

Remember, boomers grew up with their parents collecting and trading stamps. Today, nearly all boomers carry loyalty cards, and they use them. They collect loyalty points. They like coupons. They like dis- counts and don't mind taking the time to use them.

You can work that into your business. Even if your company has no coupon or gift card, there's no reason you can't create a coupon with a decent discount and a color printer.

Even if you don't have any computer skills, it's easy to outsource the job on fiverr.com so you can have somebody create a coupon for you.

If you're in an anti-aging or skin care company, you can offer a free facial. If you're in a party plan, then you have coupons for free products or discounts.

Even if you're purchasing leads, which I don't like but I'll give you this tip, you can use this coupon concept.

When I do any form of direct mail campaign, I will offer my new rep a set amount of the same list from which they came.

This concept is so important psychologically because most people will assume, which is only logical, that if they joined from a list, that list must be good.

They will ask you how you got their name because they will assume everyone on that list is like them and will join too.

Sometimes that's true, and sometimes it's not.

No matter what, nearly all the people who joined from a method feel that method is good.

It's the same when you look at a billboard that says, "You have just proved that billboards work." You haven't proven anything, or have you? Even if a thousand people drove by that sign and didn't look, our mind makes the assumption, "Yes, that's right, signs work!"

Now, you can work that psychology into your marketing.

For example, with leads I'll say, "Look, if you join me, I will give you 500 leads for free." I know these leads have a true value of x. I'd be buying 5,000 leads at a time but if somebody joined and he made a product purchase, I'd say, "I'm going to give you 500 leads. That's for free. You'll pay for the direct mail costs. I can send the package for you, or you can mail it out, but you'll get those leads free to get you started."

I could have put that into a coupon or a nice letter in my prospecting package.

Put your coupon into any package you mail out.

Coupons may be the thing that pushes your prospect over the edge. You might have emailed them, called them, sent them a postcard, but the coupon with a discount may be what nailed it.

In my early days, I would offer free sets of business cards with a value of $34, to anyone who joined with me at the 'Direct' level. I earned $1200 at that level, and the prospect knew it, but for the sake of 500 cards people often make decisions.

FYI business cards are still valued by people. Why? Because business cards have their name on them.

Today you can also pay for someone's prospecting site for three months, or some other inducement. Everyone loves a bonus or freebie. Everyone. Just put it in writing as a coupon for your boomer market.

Now, I like offering leads because by providing leads or a coupon for discounted quality leads from a good mailing list, you can have a much greater likelihood of recruiting somebody over those that don't. Coupons are great. You can create your own. You can use them for both online and offline marketing. It's an excellent tactic.

Newspapers: Boomers still read newspapers. Studies show that women boomers will read more newspapers than men. This habit is something you can factor in. If you do wish to advertise in a newspaper, put it in weekly. Weekly papers work very well.

A way to do a good sized ad is through a lead co-op because it can be expensive. The difference between the display ad over classified ads is that classifieds are those small ones often found in the back of a paper.

They work great if they run for months. A display ad is a more expensive option. A display ad can be larger, three by three or half a quarter page, whatever your paper offers.

When is the best time to advertise?

Advertising typically follows the same patterns as the best times for recruiting. Obviously not in late December. Mid-January through May and up until mid-June are good. The hot summer months are not as strong. Then, of course, starting September around Labor Day, and all the way up until mid-December. Those are the weeks and months that work the best. This timing is true for direct mail, unless you are doing a Christmas tie-in in which you can mail up until Christmas.

In general, don't mail anything out during a holiday or over the summer. It will not pull as well as it would during the top times.

TIP: If you're in a city where times are tough, go to a newspaper and see if you can make a deal. There's certainly no reason you cannot try.

Always try. While we're talking about direct mail, I want to mention that radio stations in small cities are also worth making a deal with. When you contact any kind of media, they'll send you a rate card.

Don't just assume that those rates are at face value unless you're living in New York City where they're not going to give you a deal.

If you're living in a small place where times are tough, you can negotiate and get good deals. If you're not living in a small place where times are tough, Chicago or in New York, for example, there's no reason you can't advertise in areas where times are tough.

Catalogs:

We covered catalogs in the last chapter. These work, as I wrote, very well for boomers. If your company has catalogs, excellent. If not, don't go to the expense of making your own catalog.

Advertorials

The advertorial is a powerful direct mail piece you can make yourself. Send it to a prospect, or pay to have it inserted into a magazine or paper.

You will see samples of advertorial type ads in my swipe file, which you can get by emailing me at DavidWilliamsAuthor@gmail.com and entering the words 'Swipe File' into the subject line.

As a direct mail piece, the best are those that appear to be ripped out of the newspaper and cut out, then enclosed in an envelope and mailed.

They look like actual stories or articles, yet everyone knows they are not. You write them yourself, or you can hire a copywriter to write them.

Add some pictures in and print them on newsprint or magazine stock. Cut or rip them out so the final piece appears as if they've been taken from actual newspapers or magazines.

You mail this finished piece with a sticky or a post-it note on it with a hand written message. "Hey, Bob, check this out and call me." Then add your name and phone number at the bottom as your CTA, (call to action).

Another good CTA is "Call me after you've read this."

Again, if you use a good list, this method works well. If you use a bad list, they don't work well. It's the same for all lead sources.

Now I want to cover direct mail with audio and video.

These mediums are powerful. We've talked about how boomers have a much longer attention span, and they like physical material. Most of you already have webinars and sites where you can download a video recording of your business presentation. Even if you don't have any tech savvy whatsoever to create a webinar for yourself, you can make DVDs from your company or team and download them. From there you can create a master DVD and produce copies.

It's very inexpensive to make a nice looking DVD cover if you subcontract the job on Fiverr.

A lot of people today have printers where you can print right on your DVD. I was doing that for a while. Then, I just picked up the phone and called around. Soon I found a few companies that were able to make a DVD for me. A few more calls, and I found both expensive and inexpensive companies that would literally make DVDs for me for a dollar each, including spraying my cover image onto the DVD, adding my color cover to the case, and shrink-wrapping each one for about $2 each.

It looks very professional putting your DVD in a plastic case and shrink wrapping it. If can do that and mail it out. It doesn't cost you much more than a couple of bucks each. However, the intrinsic value to the person who receives it is extremely powerful. Now, you can download one of your webinars or training. Or you can film it next time you attend one.

If you want to go the extra mile, insert yourself. Film yourself introducing your meeting and talking about why somebody should get involved with you and then introduce your webinar. When your webinar is completed, come on again. Talk about yourself and deliver a CTA.

You're using what we call bookends. You're the bookend at the beginning and end of the video.

If you read my branding book, you know that you can get good intro's and outros for your videos for $5 to $90. While they are just a few seconds long, they create a dramatic effect.

If you picked up my 'Done for YOU' branding pack, part of your pack included a personalized outro. Email me if you want a special price on the branding pack. Say you read my boomers book to get the special price.

You can put together a DVD for next to nothing. If you create a DVD and start mailing it, boomers will watch it. They'll slip it into their DVD players or computers and watch them.

You can do this for audios as well as DVD videos.

Now, if you want to get even more professional looking, you can go to companies like www.kunaki.com. They will put your DVD or CD on sale for you. You can put a price on your DVD, for example, $19.99. Someone can go online and purchase your CD or DVD video.

You can put on your marketing material or letter, "Dear Bob, I'm sending you this $29.99 video free because I value your feedback. Give me a call as soon as you've watched it."

You can make the value $49.99 or more. It's up to you because you decide the price when you upload it to kunaki.com.

Whether people buy it or not, that's the price.

If somebody wants to go on Google and look up the title, they'll find it on www.kunaki.com for sale for $49. If they want to buy it, they can. You'll get all the profit, after the cost of about three bucks. That's what www.kunaki.com will take. It doesn't cost any money to set this up with www.kunaki.com either. Just go to www.kunaki.com., read about it and you'll see.

There are other companies like Kunaki. Google 'competitors to Kunaki' to find them.

Videos work extremely well, as do CDs for Boomers. Remember CDs are just audio files. If you want to, get out there and create something that people can listen to in their cars. This tactic works very, very well. Prior to the days of CDs, we used to buy cassette tapes and duplicate them. I finally threw away my high-speed cassette duplicator since people don't use cassettes anymore.

Why did I have my own high-speed tape duplicator?

Besides using cassettes, I would make one cassette master. I would put three blank cassettes in and press a few buttons. My high-speed audio duplicator would duplicate both sides of the cassette. I would send prospects home with a cassette from my meetings, so they could listen to it in the car and we would hand out cassettes to people at stop lights in the summer.

People who were bored with radio would listen to our pitch driving home. We chose anyone in a suit. The drive from downtown would take half an hour. They would listen to our presentation. It worked fantastically. I know one person who built a huge organization with this method.

Of course, now it's different due to MP3s and downloads. CDs are slowly going the way of the cassette; however, there are still a few years left for CDs. Today CDs are very inexpensive to make, you can have them made for 50 cents or less. If you want to do it yourself, you certainly can.

Note: One of the things that will make a huge difference when creating the CD or DVD is the cover. It's not expensive to have a cover or label created for you on Fiverr.

I'm talking about the label. I'm not talking about a sticker. A nice label makes all the difference.

I've given you some excellent ideas to use Direct Marketing, and if you email me at DavidWilliamsAuthor@gmail.com for a copy of my 'DM Swipe File" I'll send you a PDF of some sample Direct Marketing Letters from all sorts of industries that you can use for ideas.

Of course, you can use any of these ideas to market to anyone, not just boomers. Boomers have a higher attention span and have more DVD and CD players than millennials. Millennials are more apt to use downloads, iPads, and smartphones for audio and videos.

Lights, Camera, Action!

The Fear Factor or Using Fear for Fun and Profit for Maximum Results

Motivation through Fear

Now, while our chapter title sounds ultra-negative, understand that most network marketing messages use fear to motivate people. In fact, all marketing is about fear versus reward.

Networkers use the concept of fearing loss, and we teach it to our teams. Once you have this concept down, it's a powerful motivator.

For example, networkers use 'fear of loss' in positioning.

Positioning?

Positioning is the term we use when we're showing somebody what starting level product purchase they might want. It's not mandatory so we need to show WHY someone would spend money when they don't have to.

"If you begin in this business with $900 in PV, you instantly qualify at the Star Trek Commander position and that means you'll earn 29% commission on all of your new business next month. If you don't (loss), then not only will you be handicapped because you won't have any samples, or be able to try the product yourself, but all of the commissions from new people you recruit and start with a product order will be passed up to me. So, it's in your best interest (reward) to get yourself a serious amount of product and get positioned to collect all those commissions next month.'

"Not only that, Bob, for your entire life in this business, each person whom you sponsor will look at you and say, "Bob, I'm going to start the way you did. How did you start?"

Most networkers use this close one way or another, and I believe in it. Even if your prospect has to stretch and borrow the money like I did when I started many years ago.

We show fear of loss. When we build interest for events, we use fear of loss too. "If you miss this event, you'll be missing out on...."

Fear of loss is: What will you lose if you don't do 'x'?

I'm going to cover the concept of fear so that you don't feel that it's a negative method.

People need to know, in real emotional terms, the consequences of an action or in-action.

Manipulation is not a bad thing – it's just a term.

A lot of people see the word and give it a bad rap because we tend to see it used in a bad way - 'she or he is a manipulator' in a relationship sense. Or 'that evil dictator manipulated their entire population to achieve their dastardly ends'.

At the same time, as parents, we've learned how to manipulate our children to do good things (reward) and our children learn how to manipulate us too. This prepares them for the world.

When we talk about manipulation, we're not talking about it in a negative way or a positive way. It's just neutral. What we are doing is showing people the consequences of taking an action or not taking an action.

Boomers

Now, let's cover what specific fears boomers have so we can show them how to avoid what they fear by engaging in our business.

The first fear stems from the fact that boomers are aging. As we grow older, we fear death. It's not as a big of a deal to younger people.

I remember once talking to a millennial who made the statement, "Well, you know, I'm 30 years younger than you are, so I'm gonna live longer."

I said, "Well, not necessarily. For example, if a meteorite came down and hit both of us now, who would have won the race of a longer life? I would have lived longer."

When we are young, we think we will live forever.

As we grow older, we have more invested in living. We know how hard it is to start over.

FYI: It's this fact that makes sponsoring boomers more profitable. They've got so much experience in business and socially that they bring a lot to the position. Teenagers think that they're running rings around their parents in terms of manipulating and telling them stories. As we grow older, we just shake our heads and think "Really? I've been there. I've been a teenager. I know what you are thinking."

Getting back to fear of death, it's not so much a fear of death per se. It's all the problems that come with aging and diseases leading to death.

For example, dying without leaving enough money for the family, that's a fear factor for boomers.

It's not for the young.

Trying to convince a twenty-two-year-old male who just got married that he wants a $5,000,000 insurance policy paid out to his wife in case of his death, is not an easy sell!

He's secretly thinking, "Gee, I've got this very attractive young wife. If I die tomorrow, do I want to make her a millionaire? Some other guy is going to come along, and they'll have a better life then we will."

Believe it or not, this is evolutionarily sound thinking. It's a base thought from deep in the reptile part of our brain. If you were an insurance agent, you'd have to be very careful with how you market that policy.

This concept is why smart agents often sell a very little insurance policy to newlyweds. They sell just enough to lock in that client-family, and then they wait for the first born.

Once that baby comes along, a male now desires that his line continues, so he has a different outlook and thinks, "It's okay. I don't mind if you're a wealthy millionairess because you've got to take care of our child. If somebody comes along and marries you and wants to raise the child, so much the better."

The next thing that we need to realize in terms of fear is how age is relative.

When you're ten years old, one year seems like a long time because it's a tenth of your life. In fact, it's less than a tenth of your life because you only have memories from when you were maybe four or five years old.

When you're twenty years old, a year is a twentieth of your life. When you're forty, one year is only a fortieth of your life. When you're sixty, one year is just a sixtieth of your life.

As we get older, a year seems to pass so much faster, relative to those younger than us.

For boomers time flies.

When I say fear of loss, rest assured your boomer understands time is money.

Just remind them, "You need some time to think, of course. Take all the time you need. Just realize that you mentioned to me the reason you're here is to build a residual income for you and your family. Something that will last if something happens to you. At our age, we've only got, ten, twenty good years in us. That's not a long time. We've got to get started today."

Returning to the topic of fear...

As we learned, boomers have a lot of time invested in their lives. Therefore, boomers tend to drink less than they did when they were younger. Boomers drive slower that others on the road. Boomers are more concerned with preserving their life. They no longer think that they will live forever.

These concerns are also why they will listen when you have a product testimonial.

Fear also crosses over into politics.

Boomers tend to be more conservative, which stretches into their voting. Typically, when people are afraid, they tend to vote conservatively, preferring the law and order ticket. I'm not saying anything negative about conservatives. It is true that the way to get elected as a conservative is to keep warning people about doom and gloom regarding crime, the economy, jobs, housing prices, and more.

"We've got a huge immigration problem coming from Mexico." Or, "The price of oil has just dropped. We've got to do something about it."

Small 'L' liberals tend to be more optimistic. If you think back about Boomers when they were younger, in the 1960's, the sexual revolution, the anti-Vietnam era, the anti-Nixon era, they were a liberal generation. Nixon was the president for the old people and the young people were against Nixon. Now they have turned into parents.

I'm not trying to weigh in on politics. Just know that no matter what political stripe you are, probability-wise, your boomers are going to be more conservative than they were when they were younger.

That doesn't mean there are no outliers. It doesn't mean they're not liberal boomers. You may be that person. It's just to know from a marketing angle that you will find a keen ear if you are offering products that deal with the fears that boomers have.

And we want to help them eliminate their fears by purchasing our products or joining our team.

Remember, all our marketing must be based on and predicted with the idea that you really can help people achieve their goal and eliminate their fears.

That's what you need to tie together when you're a marketer. Obviously, the fear of not having enough money is something boomers have.

Let's look at the MLM gold company, Karatbars, for example.

If you examine the reason people are buying gold, it's because they have a fear about their currency.

Generally speaking, the people buying gold are older than people who are not buying gold.

Karatbars is a network marketing company and affiliate program.

Fear is a part of their selling feature.

There's nothing wrong with that because their target market is boomers, who are buying gold because they fear there could be a problem with currencies, international economies, and even international conspiracies.

If I was marketing gold, that's exactly the way that I would do that. Speak about those things not to scare people – but to sell to those who are already scared.

People don't buy gold if they're not scared. Why would you buy gold if you were not scared? If you're not scared about currency, what would be the point of buying gold?

I only win when I'm buying gold if I'm scared that my currency is going to devalue. I'll feel more secure.

Remember, it's not that you go and scare people into buying gold. Look for people who are already scared about the economy.

Same as selling an anti-aging product. You don't go to young people and tell them they can 'keep their youth', you offer older people who fear the mirror a way to get their looks back.

This fear factor for prospecting and communication is a big lesson in marketing. You don't convince people they need your product. Find people already convinced they have a problem and show them how you can solve it.

If I was in Karatbars, I won't try to convince everybody that the currency is going to fall with doom and gloom on the horizon. I'll just talk about doom and gloom openly. Whoever nods their heads is a prospect.

Then I say, "Okay. Here's the solution. Invest in gold. I'm an affiliate of one of the world's largest online gold companies."

Remember, amateurs convince or sell, but professionals sort out and find people who already want what you have.

Boomers, the Work Place, and Fear

Imagine the boomer going to work and having to compete with all the younger models every day. If you're selling an anti-aging product or you're selling long term residual income that's a good message to them.

If you fear losing your job to a younger person, you're apt to want to get a Plan B started.

They fear the writing on the wall. They fear the kids they work with now are going to find a way to get rid of them.

So the boomer may join your business to hedge his bets.

In general, these types of fears and issues are common to boomers. They may not admit them to you. They may not even admit them to themselves, but those fears are there.

People don't often admit their fears to themselves, but they're still deep inside. If you show them a way to beat that fear, they unconsciously move toward your solution.

They may even deny that's what motivated them, but if they join, that's all they wanted. Fears are real for people, even the ones that are not real.

Take a look at what's being offered to boomers on a daily basis. There's a huge industry in fear mongering right now. You can find all sorts of fear-based websites.

Look at the **Drudgereport.com**, which is one of the world's ugliest websites, yet it is extremely powerful. It can manipulate US politics, news reporting, and make or break anyone. It's one of the top ten sites in the world for news. It's a whole fear mongering website; just check it out. All the worst news is there.

The guy behind it, Matt Drudge, finds all the negative news reports and links to them. Negative news is the kind people like to hear.

There's an old saying in the news industry, 'if it bleeds, it leads.' Negative news sells.

FYI: Before you ever blame the news media for raining down doom and gloom, remember they cater to human demand and what viewers make popular. People are interested in gossip and negativity.

I've often thought that an ad on the Durdgereport.com would pull well for boomers.

FYI – For your own mental health stay away from the news. Remember what Zig Ziglar says, "Don't bother with the news because it will just make you negative as well." I quite agree.

Let's look at the health industry such as where and how they spend their ad dollars. They spend it on fear.

For example, a little bit of arthritis is advertised as something that will only get worse, so consumers are encouraged to purchase the product right now. They add that if you don't make the call, the consumer could end up crippled.

Boomers have seen people who are crippled so the evidence suggests these messages are real.

If your product can help with people's arthritis, there's an issue you can address.

For the boomer, fearing the impending economy of Armageddon is an angle for you in terms of some products (i.e., gold), or just your opportunity in general, (making money).

Boomers fear running out of money before they die. There's the old joke, "I've got more month at the end of my money." This joke is true for people who are forced to retire and are going to live longer without enough money saved. These are legitimate fears.

Boomers also fear they will run out of health before they die. Most of them are not planning to quit working, but there is a fear they will be too unhealthy to work. Once that scenario is imagined, there is concern about how will they support themselves.

If you're selling something that helps somebody's health, this is an angle.

Boomers are not afraid of a quick, merciful death. They are fearful of a long lingering illness.

When you show your health products to boomers, they listen.

There are a lot of great network marketing products which will make you healthier just by taking them because of the lack of good vitamins and minerals that are in the foods we eat today. The supplement industry understands this, but you need to articulate that to boomers in terms of their fears. Learn to connect the dots to eliminate fears

Let's look at wellness products, for example.

Many boomers have no idea that the food they eat today is killing them. The nutritional quality of our food is a fraction of what it was in 1930.

Our meat is full of drugs, our fruits and vegetables are grown in nutritionally starved earth, chemicals are added to everything to extend their shelf-life, but your average boomer doesn't know that. You must find a way to connect your solution to their fears of a long and lingering painful death in a nursing home.

The nice thing about selling wellness products to boomers is the fact that they notice a difference! They respond more quickly and notice improvements.

Still I see millennials going to other millennials to try and sell their wellness products and expecting the same results that boomers report through their testimonials.

Other than people that hit the gym and health-types, I find it is so much easier have a boomer try a wellness product because he will probability notice a difference.

If you give vitamins, enzymes, and supplements to people who are in their 20's, they don't typically notice much of a difference if any.

Remember when you were 21? You could go out drinking all night and then to work the next day. But offer your product to people 50+ years old and they'll notice the change! Offer health products to boomers and you'll find at least one out of three will call you back and say, "Wow, I noticed a difference immediately."

Different networking companies have different products. Sometimes the products will just cure pain, constipation, some of them cure headaches. Some of them lower fevers. Some give you more energy in the day, others promise a decent sleep. Some are regenerative, anti-aging, anti-inflammatory, and some fill nutrition gaps. Those with a decent quality will help nearly anyone in the boomer age group.

Why not market to boomers if you have products like this if you know they notice the change and will order more?

Fear Publishing

Agora Publishing is a very big publisher, and is hugely successful. If you get on some of their mailing lists, you will learn the art of fear marketing.

Just go to Wikipedia and look up Agoria. You can see all the different products they sell, especially if you are in the supplement industry. They also offer investment advice, and it's also doom and gloom.

If you're selling gold or you're just using the fear of the economy as a reason for somebody to get involved in your network marketing company, get on some of Agoria's mailing lists. They are the experts at using fear to motivate sales.

FYI: They market to boomers and seniors.

And Even More Fears

If you want to think of a good way to sum up fear it's that age fuels fear.

As people get older, fear is a much better motivator than when they're younger. It is important to understand.

Here are a few other fears you can make note of and use for boomers:

Fear of living with chronic pain. Whether that's from arthritis or any other kind of pain, chiropractors have made use of this fear for years.

The fear of looking old means the market will be responsive to anti-aging cream.

Men feel unhappy if they think they are out of the running and women feel they are invisible after age 50. These are irrational fears, but they are real and bankable!

Fear of mentally slowing down. Anti-Aging formulas are great to market to those of us who feel we're not thinking as fast as we once were; we need to keep up.

Fear of Legal Issues

Companies like Legal Shield, or other pre-paid legal products, work better with older people because as we age, we not only have more to lose, we have seen more of our contemporaries lose assets through the legal system.

Newspapers seem full of stories about how many people get sued and lose all their assets, where young people don't even notice articles like this in the media.

Fear of being hospitalized is something we have covered, but it's worth re-stating this, "Hey if you maintain your health, your chance of a long hospital stay will substantially decrease."

The fear of being wiped out by the cost of a long hospital stay is important.

Fear of being a victim of crime also increases as we age, even though crime is lower today than it ever was. This increase in fear is partly due to the news media, and partly due to having more to lose.

If your company sells security items, the fear of robbery is much greater as we grow older, creating a market for this product. I'm sure you have seen the alarm companies focus their sales to boomers. If you ever see the ads on TV for security companies, notice that there tend to be older models in the ads.

This is true for cybercrime as well. Younger people don't have this fear as much as boomers. Boomers have more in their bank accounts than younger people do, which is more to lose.

Another fear is our weight.

Younger people worry more about their weight because they fear they will be unloved and not have sex appeal. Boomers fear it because of health as well as sex appeal.

Of course, if you have a weight-loss product, then it's universal. It works for everybody no matter what their age. If you're sixty-five, it's often about health but if you're twenty, it's mostly about looks.

Health, as I say again, to a twenty-year-old, is not a big concern. If you bring it up, you'll get a "Yeah, whatever."

To sum up our fear factor chapter:

Age increases fear. Age fuels fear.

If you can offer a solution to a fear people secretly have, you're going to be extremely successful in our industry.

Stress and the Rule of 72 – You don't know this one

Remember when you were young, or if you are still in your twenties or thirties, remember when you loved stress? It made life real, and we thrived on it. Stress was good.

Boomers see stress differently now. Stress kills. Doctors say this, so it must be true. Multi-tasking is no longer as easy, and anyone pushing you to make a decision is maddening.

If you're selling to boomers, lead with how your product will remove stress from their life.

If your compensation plan is complex, don't go into all the details of the Star Commander Bonus that only applies two levels down through four generations of personally enrolled preferred customers on the bi-month family pack auto ship program.

In fact, don't even tell me about it.

Decision making takes longer as we age, therefore if you're marketing to boomers, don't push them into making an instant decision. We obviously want people to make quick decisions, but we want to be sure that they have the time to make that decision.

A younger person will make a decision faster, so don't think if a boomer is delaying or taking longer to make a decision, it's because they're not interested.

The Rule of 72

Your job is to keep connecting with them while they make the decision because there's a rule of 72 in network marketing. Within 72 hours, people will forget about your opportunity. Find a way to keep it at the front of their mind through e-mail, phone call, voicemail, letter, postcard, whatever method you chose. Doing that will keep their minds on making that decision.

By the way, the rule of 72 applies to all ages, but it's a must for boomers.

⭐ Critical

Decisions and Product Orders

In terms of decisions and stress, are initial product orders. It's much better to have a sample product order for people – especially boomers.

Boomers expect you to have solid suggestions. So they will listen to your positioning strategy. If the best positon for someone to start at in your company is with $900 worth of products, show it to them and explain why with details. Show the different advantages.

Don't sound apologetic or you are sending a mixed message, and boomers will pick up on that faster than the younger crowd. Once you have them agreeing to the logic for starting at that level, then show your sample product order, but use a different term for it. For example, instead of calling it a sample-product-order, try calling it something like 'Smart Start-up Pack'.

If you just hand a boomer an empty order form and said fill it out on your own, you may just lose them.

Decision-making gets more and more difficult as we grow older, and you'll embarrass older boomers if you leave it to them. Remember, we covered that boomers respect authority, experts, and specialists. That's you. So demonstrate it by showing leadership, this removes stress.

FYI: This is why leadership in all forms is one of the few things scarce in our world today.

All you need to do is help people make those decisions by offering them a templated decision made for them.

Options are bad. When presented with too many options, boomers, more than most, will get that 'deer in the headlights kind' of stare.

I hate giving options to people in any market unless I must. Unless it's just one or two things, and I always hedge my bets by pushing one particular option.

The best way to sell something is to show two inferior things next to what you want the person to purchase. This is not a negative manipulation. It's a positive one because people don't know what products to start with.

People are relying on you. Don't say, "Well, I'm going to leave it up to you. It's your business, and only you know what you sell."

Boomers don't know what to start with, nor does anybody. Boomers, more than millennials, will want and need your advice.

Be sure you choose correctly for them. I don't mean choosing for yourself. Choose the right option for them.

Bottom line: eliminate stress from within your business, not just in your marketing message. This bottom line is especially true when dealing with the boomer market. You will start seeing your boomer distributor bringing their friends to see you too.

critical

c

10 Reason's that boomers are the best prospects

Boomers are the perfect prospects.

First of all, many boomers want and desire money. I'm not just talking about the ones who literally need money. Due to the sheer fact of their age, most boomers recognize that no matter how much money they have, you cannot be overly prepared. And they want to be more prepared.

Boomers are great at saving for a rainy day and have lived long enough to see that rainy days do come along. That same desire makes them seek out and acquire more money.

While some may be broke, Boomers often have funds to start a business. They take that business much more seriously than millennials.

Recently, I read how one million dollars is no longer considered to be a safe amount of money for peace of mind. Now you need 5 million. This change is due to the deep devaluation of money since boomers were born.

Being a millionaire today is no longer a big deal. Some people's homes are worth a million dollars or half a million dollars, and yet they are certainly not in that same millionaire status as, 'Thurston Howell, III – of Gilligan's Island." (See that? It was a frame of reference connection.)

Even boomers who have seen their homes increase in value know that they still must have cash flow - even if they own their home outright.

They need money, and they are looking to make more money.

The next reason that they are the perfect niche is the fact that they are bored at that age. Boomers are no longer being tested. They are no longer able to do something of value, and they are looking to do something with their lives.

You can only play so many games of golf or bridge, and you can only travel to the beach so much. Eventually it all comes back down to this whole concept of retirement. What does that even mean?

If a boomer hated their job, retirement is a blessing, for a while. After all those years of work, they are ready to do something, but what?

Some will find hobbies such as painting, crafts, music or even going back to college. Many have 'business' minds. Those are your prospects.

The reality is that boomers, especially those who were white collar or middle management, are looking to do something with their lives. They want to use their minds. Don't think that because somebody has money that they are not bored silly.

They are going crazy. Now there are two of them at home when before there may only have been one. They are looking to do something to get out of the house.

You need to realize that having a business at home doesn't necessarily mean as much to a boomer as it does to somebody who wants to stop going to work to avoid a long commute.

You have to build your marketing around your prospect; not your 'one size fits all' kind of marketing.

Boredom is a really big reason boomers are a good market. Ignore them and someone else will recruit your boomer prospect.

Reason number 3 is boomers are experienced.

They obviously have more experience than millennials. They have more experience with human beings and more experience in buying and selling. They've seen more things happen in life so that they understand preparedness. They understand people dying from lack of concern for their health, and they'll understand people being in trouble for not saving.

Experience gives them the ability, and they are looking to make use of it. Boomers understand people being in trouble for not working hard, and they recognize these things. You are speaking to the right people when you talk about hard work and provide rewards for working hard.

If you hear a prospect, say to you, "Look. I'm happy, I'm retired. I don't need something like this." Then that's fine. Stop pushing your business on them, and sell some product. Look for the person who is experienced, bored and looking for an opportunity. Offer with an opening such as, "Bob, Mary, you got so much experience. It's just a shame to waste it."

The number 4 reason is boomers have been pushed aside by others.

This is the common enemy factor we've talked about before. Remember, you need to know who your prospect's enemy is. In this case, a lot of boomers may see the enemy as the younger generation that demanded they leave their jobs to make room.

"Get out of the lifeboat, we have our lives to lead now, it's our turn."

This is how many boomers see their last years on the job. Those boomers needed those jobs or felt they did.

There are a number of reasons for this, of course. Younger people want to get that promotion and the pay raise that goes with it. Some see boomers as hanging around until they are age 65 or 67, just trying to get as much of a pension as they possibly can.

Of course, boomers feel negative about that, and they will resent those people who have pushed them aside. You can offer them an opportunity where people work together, and back-stabbing or brown-nosing has no value.

The 5th reason is boomers have a bigger network.

Boomers are connected people and the people who they are connected to have money. Plus they have all the other advantages we've discussed.

Networking is all about utilizing somebody else's network.

Number 7 is that boomers respond well to longer presentations.

Those of us in network marketing are prone to talk too long sometimes. You can build a longer presentation, take the time to explain what you do. That tactic works very well with this market. For boomers, the more you tell, the more you sell.

Number 8 is that boomers respond well to DVDs and direct mail.

In the world where the electronic gatekeeper is king, it is hard to bust through it in our marketing.

Reaching prospects is getting tougher and tougher. Direct mail is making a comeback. That means sending letters, postcards, lumpy mail, DVDs, audio CDs, and samples.

Sending these to boomers is not as expensive as you think, especially when you're target market is people who are interested and have the money to start at a decent level.

Number 9 is the fact that it is easy to market through fear to boomers.

There are a number of network marketing companies that will help lower the fears and stresses of boomers. Many form products that help their health, as well as products that help their finances. Think of those that sell insurance, gold, etc.... For stress, think of essential oils.

Number 10 is the fact that boomers work very hard and they are reliable.

These are good people. If you think about recent meetings you've attended you'll see that a large group in the audience are boomers. It just makes sense, and you need to target your market to this niche.

FYI: An example of wrong marketing is people still talking about the 40 40 40 plan. Especially when I see this aimed at millennials. Millennials don't understand what you mean by the 40 40 40 plan. You work 40 years for $40,000 to get a $40 gold watch at the end of it all.

First of all, $40,000 is not a lot of money anymore. Nobody thinks of $40,000 as a goal, and nobody works 40 years in one job these days.

And as far as a gold watch, millennials don't even wear watches!

Boomers know that the 40-40-40 plan hasn't been around for a number of years, so you only look silly bringing it up. Get smart and get some boom into your business by recruiting within the boomer niche.

Boomers tend to do what they are told and they want to know what to do. Contrast this with 'know it all' millennials!

They do follow advice as long as they are on your side, and they trust and respect you.

If your product or opportunity fits into any of the needs of boomers then build a marketing plan for your business, targeting the 'best of all niches' category.

Contact me anytime if you have questions,

Best, David

And get on my mailing list – go to www.DavidWilliamsMLMauthor.com to join – its free, and I provide updates on all of my material, don't delay, get over there now and join.

Boomers by the Numbers

In part 2, I cover more about the background for boomers, so you can get a good general idea about this important niche.   It is less 'marketing' and more background, good for grounding yourself in the mindset of this group, as well as the different sub-groups within.

I also cover the historical background that is shared by boomers, and that's useful to read over as you prepare your 'framing'.

What is the Back-Story on "Baby Boomers"?

Between 1946 and 1964, there were 76 million births in the United States—a cohort representing the largest generation of Americans ever been born in this country. The volcanic birth explosion reflected the post-World War II national mood of confidence, as male veterans (and women who had been provided jobs to support the war effort) experienced the surging American economic growth resulting from the destruction of European and Japanese economies.

But, let's back up to consider the societal changes occurring across the United States following the global conflagration that left over 60 million dead. In the early 1950s, all the "Rosie the Riveter" girls were strongly encouraged to leave their jobs to enable the veterans to resume their traditional, civilian, bread-winner roles.

These hard-working young adult women were exhorted to—as soon as possible—become wives and mothers. They were barraged with propaganda films that depicted their natural roles in a utopian setting where men worked, women were "stay-at-home moms", and suburban home ownership (with a backyard and dog named "Spot") was the nuclear family goal.

According to a 2014 report by the U.S. Census Bureau, there were two features that distinguished this particular birth cohort from others that occurred before or after—the size of the cohort, and the length of time (19 years in total) that this unusually high fertility rate was sustained; the peak was reached in 1957 with 4.3 million births (1). Additionally, the entire age structure of the United States population shifted by the 1960s to a younger overall demographic.

Now, let's jump ahead to the present (or at least to the 21st century) to understand the effect of this birthrate on the total U.S. population. In 2011 (when the first "Baby Boomers" turned 65 years old)—and within a total pop. of around 310 million—there were more than 77 million "Baby Boomers" (per a United States Census Bureau report) (2). The total population as of 2014 (when the last of the "Baby Boomer" cohort turned 50 years old) was close to 319 million—and 76.4 million were "Baby Boomers". And, this sub-population is still around one-quarter of the whole U.S. population!

So, how did this cohort as a generation become known as "Baby Boomers"? The term was actually coined by advertising professionals in the 1950s and 1960s in recognition of the spending power of this enormous youth cohort.

Leading-Edge "Baby Boomers" versus Other "Baby Boomers

Please pause a moment. This book is concerned with LEB (leading-edge "baby boomers")—those who are in late middle-age rather than those who are seniors. Persons born before 1951 are facing their senior years (and the concomitant issues that face seniors in the United States). But, LEB individuals (born between 1951 and 1964) are not yet eligible as a group for Medicare and Social Security—or even the early Social Security benefits allowed at age 62. They are still professionals, politically influential in their neighborhoods and nationally, building economic resources for their later years—and are an enormous, potent market for goods and services.

The sub-group of "Baby Boomers" who were born in 1951 or earlier were finishing high school or college at the time of Woodstock and massive hitch-hiking. They are closely associated with the culture of the 1960s. They clearly remember segregation in the South—along with Walter Cronkite's news reports of American military deaths in Viet Nam, the institutionalization of homosexuals as mentally ill, and the lack of effective contraception to prevent pregnancy (plus illegality of abortions).

In contrast, LEB individuals were mostly adolescents (or younger) during the height of the 1960s "hippie" era—not to mention during the violent confrontations in the South over voting rights for African Americans, and end of the ban on interracial marriages. These historical occurrences in the 1960s were something their older siblings and friends ingrained in their collective memories, but they did not generally experience these defining events "first-hand".

Instead, most LEB individuals matured into the "hey-day" time period of self-exploration and consciousness-raising that permeated the 1970s. The byword in the 1970s was "pride"—whether Black pride, Gay pride, or the pride emanating from the Women's Liberation Movement.

What is my point? It's just to express that there was actually a difference between the cultural experiences of the earlier half of the "Baby Boomer" cohort from the later half. The focus of the remaining chapters of this book is on those "Baby Boomers" who came of age in the 1970s or 1980s. The slogan of the 1960s was "never trust anyone over 30". For the LEB individuals—emerging into young adulthood with unlimited opportunities—it seemed that old age would never happen to them. They would remain youthful forever, and sixty would be the new forty.

What Drives Boomers?

The Similarities and Differences Based on Gender

Unlike their parents—the "Greatest Generation"—the "Baby Boomers" grew up during a time period of continuous economic growth and with governmental "safety nets" in place (following passage of President Lyndon Johnson's "Great Society" legislation). Johnson's anti-poverty programs—such as food and housing aid—ensured that lack of income did not have to result in an utter catastrophe. This made it possible for those between the ages of 18 and 21 to move far from their parents (and hometowns), or to "drop out" of college to travel the world or volunteer. The 1970s saw the development of numerous "back to the land" communes, ashrams, and other communal living experiments across the country—of which The Farm in Tennessee (founded by Stephen Gaskin) was the largest.

Beginning in 1965, Volunteers in Service to America (VISTA) enabled young adults to work for a stipend in poverty programs—and inspired social idealism. In fact, "Baby Boomers" are highly represented among volunteers to nonprofits, charities, churches, and synagogues. According to the Corporation for National and Community Service, "Baby Boomers" accounted for 22% to 46% of all volunteers across all states between 2009-2011. In contrast, "Millenials" only account for 14% to 37% of volunteers across all states (3).

"What about 'Baby Boomers' attitudes toward employment?" you might ask.

In general, the idea that loyalty to a company and employer would not result in an increased salary and future economic security was a foreign concept. Even possessing only a high school diploma could ensure a decent job and paycheck (with a pension). Individuals in this cohort were intent on discovering their particular interests and talents, and in making a difference in the world. Therefore, saving money for future retirement was not a high priority in young adult-hood.

Now that this cohort is middle-aged, the label of "Sandwich Genera-tion" is often applied as a general characterization. This is due to the fact that LEB "Boomers" have become sandwiched between taking care of their parents and their grown children. No experience is more shared by these individuals than this grueling burden. Do listen up. This is such a critical aspect of the "Boomer" experience that it is one of the primary "drivers" of all major decisions for the majority of people in this demographic—especially for women in this age group.

Consumerism and Economic Anxiety about Old Age

There are two other "drivers" for this LEB population as a whole worth noting. The first is historically-based, and began in their (or our) childhoods. This was the enormous growth and expansion of manufacturing plants in the United States. Intensive marketing was directed at "Baby Boomers" to consume large appliances, home-care equipment, record albums, tobacco products, canned and pre-packaged food items, and a wide range of other American-made consumables. This tendency toward high consumption of material goods remains a trend among aging "Baby Boomers" as compared to their parents' generation. According to a 2012 article in Forbes Magazine, "Baby Boomers" as a group annually spend approximately $7 billion (and nearly 63% of all new cars are purchased by this age demographic) (4).

The second "driver" is anxiety about economic security in old age. It is widely recognized that—collectively—"Baby Boomers" did not take saving money for their senior years seriously. On the other hand, they were taught in young adulthood that retirement at around 65 years old would usher in their "golden years" (which was true for many members of the previous generation). The result is that the "nest eggs" of "Baby Boomers" are not likely, in their senior years, to cover the overall costs associated with their lifestyles. Additionally, unexpected changes in the national economy and decrease in "safety net" programs are feeding this cohort's anxieties about economic security in their old age.

While there are many similarities in what "drives" members of the LEB cohort, there are also some definite differences between males and females. The actual burden of being "sandwiched" between the needs of elderly parents or relatives, and grown-up children is one example. But, there are other significant differences.

What drives "Boomer" women?

The 1960s youth slogan of "never trust anyone over 30" had a pervasive and long-lasting effect on "Boomer" women as they aged—including the LEB cohort. Youth culture decidedly reigned supreme in the 1960s and 1970s. Consequently, "Baby Boomer" women are concerned with appearing youthful. There's a "good" side and a "bad" side to worshipping youth. Unlike the women of the "Greatest Generation", this generation of women embraced fitness and athletic activities—leading to a better health status. On the other hand, it also led to a love affair with hair dye and cosmetic surgery. "Baby Boomer" women spend a great deal of time and money attempting to look younger than their age.

Peggy Lee sang, "I can bring home the bacon, fry it up in the pan" in her hit 1960s single, entitled I'm a Woman (and this same song was recorded later by Maria Muldaur) (5). The song's refrain was adopted by advertisers in the 1970s targeting women. It captured the self-perception of LEB women—as well as the societal expectation of them. Unlike their mothers, LEB women had more career options, and were more likely to work full-time in professions. This drove the need for time-saving appliances, food items, disposable diapers, and daycare centers. These women simply had less time to focus on home and family. They were too busy proving themselves as working professionals, and attempting to break into the overwhelming number of male-dominated careers (such as television news-casting, engineering, college-level teaching, and medicine).

What drives "Boomer" men?

"Baby boomer" men have been driven mostly by a deep-seated need to economically provide for their families and children. The importance of a career and work in the lives of men within this cohort cannot be over-emphasized. Yet, the purpose of earning money has largely been tied to pride in being able to increase their overall class status for the sake of their family members. The lack of a college degree did not prevent "blue collar" men from attaining entrance into the "middle class" for decades. Meanwhile, men in "white collar" jobs focused on advancing in their careers, in their decisions to purchase homes in more affluent neighborhoods, and their hobbies (as networking tools for upward mobility).

There are thousands of sociological and psychological studies that have linked the role of work to the development of adult male "identity". However, men in traditionally "middle-class" jobs differ in the level of importance ascribed to that identity than men in traditionally "working class" jobs (e.g., floor workers in factories, custodians, and "blue collar" laborers). As previously mentioned, LEB men in professional work roles demonstrated a high level of loyalty to their employers, and a belief that their future pensions would grow and be secure. For men in "working class" jobs, labor union membership and activism represented the path to better pay, fringe benefits, and working conditions.

In 1979—the peak year for union membership throughout the United States—there were an estimated 21 million labor union members (as compared to 15 million in 2003) (6). Not only did "blue-collar" Boomer employees participate in unions in the auto industry, food processing plants, and clothing manufacturing sites, but "white collar" Boomers were also members. In 1978, Title VII of the Civil Service Reform Act enabled federal employees to unionize (6), while ACSME (the American Federation of State, County, and Municipal Employees) was building membership among state workers and university employees. In turn, the increased wages and benefits garnered by the labor unions allowed "Boomer" men to buy larger houses, better cars, and afford private school (and college tuition) for their children.

Golf has long represented the hobby of privileged men in professions—and the golf course was often where professional men could form relationships with supervisors and co-workers that could be an asset in their work-life. "Boomer" men embraced golf as a hobby in large numbers—and drove the creation and financial support of golf courses. Nearly 12 million "Baby Boomers" play golf—or around early 15% of this age demographic (according to the website of Frugal Retirement Living) (8). The amount of money spent on golf by this age demographic is huge—but it is decreasing among the "Millennials" due to their generation-wide financial burdens.

Other widely-recognized hobbies of LEB men have fueled the American economy—such as attendance at baseball and football games (and as a consumer market for televised sports events such as the World Series or Super Bowl). Like their female counterparts, "Boomer" males were raised in a consumer-oriented national environment. The purchase of late-model automobiles—and the capacity to own a recreational vehicle or yacht—were visible signs of prosperity for "Baby Boomer" men (as well as objects of enjoyment) that drove their consumerism.   The lack of ability to acquire these "status-associated" material goods has also caused them angst—especially following the Wall Street crash and attendant credit crisis in 2008. Similar to female "Boomers", it has been difficult for these men to scale back their consumer tendencies and material aspirations.

Examining the Daily Life of Leading-Edge "Boomers"

There really is no monolithic experience of "Baby Boomers"—despite the best attempts of the mass media to pigeon-hole this sub-population. This is equally true of leading-edge "Baby Boomers" (LEB) as the individuals at the older edge of this demographic. Besides gender differences, race, ethnicity, and class all impact the experience of daily life.

In terms of race, 72% of all native-born Boomers were white as of 2012 (as compared to 63% for the United States population as a whole) (9). On the other hand, the United States is a nation of immigrants, and aging parents have accompanied many younger immigrants to this country. It needs to be emphasized that these immigrants are citizens or permanent residents—and paying the same taxes as everyone else.

My point is that there are major differences in terms of concerns and needs between native-born LEB individuals and their immigrant counterparts. For example, a crucial difference is in language prefer-ence and comfort. While there is widespread acknowledgment of the increase in Hispanic and Latino individuals across the United States, the sociological focus has largely been on younger immigrants and their families. Older immigrants have been rendered far more invisible in society.

Data from the U.S. Census documents that the African American population was 44,456,009 in 2012 (or 14% of the entire U.S. popu-lation)—and up from 43,213,173 in 2010. Among African American males, 47% were between the ages of 35-64. Among African American females, 53% were between the ages of 35-64. Thirty-nine percent of male African Americans were age 65 or older; 61% of female African Americans were age 65 or older (10). This means that African American "Boomers" are a sub-population of LEBs that have race-based issues which need to be considered.

Education

The parents of LEB "Boomers" instilled a value that obtaining a four-year college degree was the ticket to lifetime employment and a "middle-class" lifestyle. Most state colleges were not that expensive when this cohort attended college. Indeed, the completion of a four-year college program generally resulted in recruitment into well-paying fields. As this cohort has aged, advances in technology have required many to obtain additional computer skills in their middle-age.

Additionally, they promote college matriculation as a "ticket" to their children—regardless of the changed economic landscape that has caused college to be an expensive "right of passage" that no longer guarantees entry into a profession for Millenials. "Baby Boomer" parents have spent a great deal of their savings to help their children afford post-high school educational cost (or acted as legal collaterals on student loans), and this is a major drain on their the financial resources.

Housing

The housing "bubble" that burst in 2006 had a terrible impact on leading edge "Baby Boomers" (LEBs). Like their parents, this generation assumed that the value of their houses would increase over time. Indeed, homeownership was a fundamental symbol of "middle-class" status—and major part of the American Dream. Until residential property values dramatically sank, LEBs were not particularly worried about their lack of savings. They viewed their home as their primary financial asset (that would fund their future retirements).

In addition, many "Baby Boomers" were duped into assuming reverse mortgages and second mortgages. They were no longer able to rely on deriving a substantial dollar amount from the sale of their properties as a bulwark against financial anxiety about growing "old".

Like the uncertainty facing young adults following the 2008 credit crisis and subsequent Recession, LEBs found themselves facing an unanticipated national misfortune. But, unlike their offspring, this cohort of "Baby Boomers" did not have the working years left to recoup the "hit" to their retirement accounts and assets—while facing a high tax burden. Images of retirement at age 65 vanished for them. Instead, many of these "Baby Boomers" have had to face the prospect of never being able to retire or enjoy "golden years".

Employment

The most intractable problem for "Baby Boomers" in employment has been age discrimination. Even without the Recession, the "prime" employment age has been considered to be between 25 and 40 years old. While younger persons may have difficulty obtaining well-paying jobs, individuals over 40 also are at a disadvantage in job-hunting. The Recession that began in December of 2007 and ended in June of 2009 caused a huge increase in unemployment (displacing over 8 million workers) (11). As has been widely acknowledged, the labor market has still not fully recovered—and hourly wages remain depressed. This is especially true for "Baby Boomers" who experienced job loss.

In 2009, the New York Times reported that unemployed workers over age 45 were disproportionately among the long-term unemployed—and that it took them in 2008 (on average) over 22 weeks to obtain new employment as compared to 16 weeks for their younger counterparts (12).

The combined effect of widespread home devaluation (resulting for a sizeable population in "under-water" mortgages or home foreclosure) with an inability to obtain employment has forced many "Boomers" into poverty—never mind out of the "middle class". After losing their faith in the absolute value of loyalty to an employer (and the ability of hiring managers to recognize their worth), these individuals are struggling to adapt to the changed times while facing the normal issues associated with middle-age.

Vacation and Travel

"Baby Boomers" are travelers. Hitch-hiking was commonplace when this cohort was coming of age, and airfare was far less expensive than at present. Many attended colleges or accepted job offers far from home—or just relocated to experience a different locale. Whatever the reason, "Boomers" have gotten used to traveling for both work and pleasure. Unlike their parents, this cohort was also more interested in experiencing foreign cultures.

Also unlike members of the "Greatest Generation", many "Boomers" in the United States are divorced or single (due to the reduced stigma associated with not being married). Therefore, they are highly represented in group travel—and vacation in more exotic locales than previous generations. As an environmentally-conscious generation, eco-tourism developed in response to their interest in visiting such unique places as the Galapagos Islands and the rainforest of Costa Rica.

The national parks are a frequent destination for family travel with children (with Yellowstone National Park as the foremost choice). This is a generation that participated in school physical fitness activities, as a result of President Kennedy and President Johnson's support for physical education in public schools. Camping in a tent with children was not viewed as only something to be undertaken by persons who could not afford a hotel—but a fun adventure for the whole family.

Since volunteering has played a major role in the earlier lives of "Baby Boomers", vacations that involve volunteer work are attractive to them, as well. Founded in 1976, Habitat for Humanity became well known when former President Carter and Rosalyn Carter took their first "work trip"—and it has remained particularly popular with "Boomers" since then.

Fitness

"Baby Boomer" women are oriented toward health and fitness far more than their mothers. Jane Fonda has been a particular inspiration to women of this demographic, since her first work-out video was released in 1982. As a 77 year-old fitness guru, she continues to demonstrate that women can preserve their physical attractiveness in later life. Due to the high rate of "Baby Boomer" divorce, many middle-aged women are dating—and still concerned about their appearance in the eyes of potential mates. Keeping "fit" is one component of preserving attractiveness for these women, and they also understand its health benefits.

Volunteering and Teaching English as a Foreign Language

"Baby Boomers" have travelled overseas to teach English in record numbers. In the 1980s, individuals living in other countries sought instruction in English as a means to increasing their economic circumstances (and/or acquiring admission to universities in the United States). In the United States, short certificate programs in Teaching English as a Foreign/Second Language took sprang up like daisies in major urban areas.

By teaching English in volunteer programs, LEB "Boomers" were able to lower the costs associated with an overseas vacation. The Internet changed the necessity of having "on-site" English teachers in foreign countries (and airfare increased), so the market diminished for sponsoring Americans to teach English in foreign schools.

Small Business Owners

According to an article on the Wealth Management.com website, there are 12 million "Baby Boomers" who own small businesses (13). This includes home-based businesses. This same article on the Wealth Management.com website suggests that 70% will be retiring in the next two decades—with a huge potential market for interested buyers and financial planners.

The cost of keeping up with the latest technology is presenting an obstacle for "Baby Boomer" business owners. For members of this age demographic who assumed management of longstanding family businesses, their need to rely on web-designers and LAN specialists presents a different type of challenge than experienced by their parents. Meanwhile, some are being rendered obsolete by online businesses that can offer the same service. For example, small businesses specializing in tax preparation have suffered due to the availability of tax software such as TurboTax and TaxAct.

Overall Spending Habits of "Baby Boomers"

In terms of purchasing consumer goods and services, this population "outspends" any other generation by approximately $400 B each year—and over 50% of all vacation dollars are spent by this cohort. Additionally, female "Boomers" spend around $21 B on clothing each year. Meanwhile, 21% of "Boomers" reported having spent more than $10,000 on home improvements in the last year (14).

Psychological Issues Affecting Leading-Edge "Boomers"

In the book entitled, Marketing to the Mindset of Boomers and Their Elders and published in 2002, the authors describe four specific personality traits within the "Baby Boomer" cohort that businesses need to consider when marketing to them (15). These are: 1) upbeat enjoyers; 2) insecures; 3) threatened actives; and 4) financial positives. While the focus is on "Baby Boomers", these personality traits are not specific to them. For this reason, I will discuss the unique psychological issues that affect the sub-population of "Baby Boomers" at the core of this book.

The Role of Caregiving

The perception of this cohort as the "Sandwich Generation" has already been introduced. But, it needs to discussed in terms of its overall psychological impact on this sub-population of "Baby Boomers". Because of medical advances that have prolonged the average lifespan, caregiving for elders is simply a huge focus of this cohort (whether those elders are parents, other relatives, or friends).

Assisted living has been marketed to the children of elders as an attractive option in later life to avoid "taking in" these elders or placing them in nursing homes. However, neither assisted living nor nursing homes are good options in terms of monthly cost. The average monthly cost is $6,235 for a semi-private room in a nursing home—while the average monthly cost for a assisted living in a one-bedroom unit is $3,923 (per the U.S. Department of Health and Human Services) (16).

Most offspring do not want to move their elderly parent into a nursing home unless it is absolutely necessary. Therefore, keeping the elderly parent or relative in their home—or finding a suitable assisted living residence—is something that many "Baby Boomers" attempt to do. Locating an acceptable assisted living unit is just one part of the stress these "Baby Boomer" experience. The second is that they often end up contributing toward assisted living expenses on behalf of the parent (especially if the parent has already contributed their entire financial "nest egg"). For many other "Baby Boomers", moving their parent into assisted living is just not a financially-viable option.

The other slice of bread that is squeezing these "Baby Boomers" is a result of the tough economic times and college debt incurred by their young adult children. Unable to acquire full-time employment—or earning a lower wage than necessary to rent an apartment—their children are returning home to live in record numbers. Therefore, instead of becoming "empty-nesters" in middle-age, many "Baby Boomer" couples are still engaged in caring for their grown children. Thirty-six percent of "Millennials" live with their parents (instead of in their own apartments) according to the Pew Research Center (17).

The psychological and financial stress experienced by the LEB "Boomers" caught between caring for elderly parents and children is immense. On top of this burden, most of these "Boomers" are working 9-5 jobs. Consequently, this cohort is continuously seeking ways to increase their available "free time" and energy level. From hiring household help to ordering "take-out" dinners and pizza to ingesting vitamin supplements, these people attempt to be "Superwoman" and "Superman" every day. Yes, they are stressed out—and they don't have the time or patience for lengthy marketing pitches – instead sell them on getting out of this stress.

Psychotherapy and "Baby Boomers"

Key!

Unlike their parents' generation, "Baby Boomers" do not experience the same high level of stigma at seeking mental health care (18). However, health insurance companies have been reluctant to cover the costs of mental health care, or limit the provider options. Even with the Mental Health Parity and Addiction Equity Act of 2008 requiring legal compliance from health insurers, it is still difficult for many insured Americans to get their carriers to pay for their psychotherapy visits.

The Impact of the Vietnam War

A large number of Vietnam War veterans (and Vietnam Era vets based in Laos and Thailand) suffered PTSD following their military service. Unlike the veterans of other wars, these Americans felt particularly unappreciated for their service on return to civilian life.

Many also returned addicted to heroin (due to the high potency and easy availability of Vietnam heroin).

While the LEB "Boomer" cohort was mostly too young to serve in that war, many had older siblings, friends, or lovers who were Vietnam veterans. Approval for PTSD-based Supplemental Social Security (SSI) benefits took years for these distressed veterans.

Because of the media focus on Iraq and Afghanistan war veterans, it is easy to forget that Vietnam Era veterans (and their family members) are still dealing with the effects. Forty-seven percent of all homeless veterans are Vietnam Era veterans (and over 50% are African Americans), according to the National Coalition for the Homelessness (19).

Divorce Impact on Baby Boomers

No doubt you are already aware that the national divorce rate is rather high. Betsey Stevenson and Justin Wolfers—in their book chapter, Trends in Marital Stability (in the esteemed Research Handbook on the Economics of Family Law—report their findings that a divorce rate was highest among "Boomers" (as compared to their parents' OR the generation that followed the "Boomers") (20). In other words, at any age, "Boomers" were more likely to have marriages that ended in divorce. The authors also suggest that the reason that younger individuals apparently have a lower divorce is because they delayed, and were more cautious about entering in marriage in the first place.

Please take a deep breath. According to the U.S. Bureau of Labor Statistics, 84% of "Baby Boomers" were married by age 46. However, 45% of these individuals (born between 1957-1964) have had at least one divorce (21). This is in significant contrast to the following generation (as well as their parents). Apparently, the divorce rate is rising NOT because of young adult divorces, but because "Baby Boomers" are still experiencing high divorce rates in middle-age. Explanations that have been suggested for the high incidence are that "Boomers" entered young adulthood during a time of tremendous change in gender roles and the importance ascribed to marriage.

"Baby Boomer" women with children who are divorced (or never married)—as a whole—experienced, in their thirties, economic stress in locating adequate childcare resources with little societal support. In the circumstances of a joint custody, these mothers also dealt with the stress resulting from their school-age children living between two homes. Meanwhile, "Baby Boomer" men experienced economic stress due to the burden of child support. This is besides the emotional stress experienced by the divorced individuals and their children.

"Baby Boomers" and Dating

Whether due to divorce or the death of a spouse, "Baby Boomers" are as likely to date and marry as any other age group. On the other hand, body image is not as important—and the ability to relate well with each other's children (as step-parents) can strongly impact the relationship. In contrast to members of the "Greatest Generation", many "Boomers" chose not to have children or postponed child-bearing until a later age. For these individuals, becoming a step-parent can involve an enormous lifestyle adjustment. Meanwhile, whether due to divorce or the death of a spouse, male "Boomers" are more likely to want to re-marry, and less comfortable with envisioning themselves living alone permanently. In contrast, many middle-aged women embrace living alone, and view this as an opportunity to focus on "self".

"Boomer" Health and Housing Concerns, Needs, and Wants

The fragmented healthcare system in the United States is a clear burden on leading-edge "Boomers", and health insurance costs weigh heavily on this cohort. Guess what? Health insurance premiums are often higher for middle-aged individuals than younger policy-holders. Additionally, the risk of health disorders and disability increases with age. According to the American Association of Retired Persons (AARP), sufficient caregiving capacity by family members (as well as long-term care services) is unlikely to be available to "Boomers" in their old age—causing a huge worry to this LEB cohort (22).

Cardiovascular Disease and "Baby Boomers"

The American Heart Association reports that—among 49-59 year olds—cardiovascular disease affects 40% of males and 34% of females. In 60-79 year olds, 70% of both genders have this life-threatening disorder (23). Heart disease is the major cause of death in the United States, and cardiovascular disease increases the risk of both heart disease and stroke. Meanwhile, smoking and obesity increase the risk of developing heart disease.

Cancer and "Baby Boomers"

One—out of every three—people will develop cancer. But, the risk is not spread evenly among all age groups. Seventy percent of all cancers develop in persons over 60 years old (24). Because of the population size of the LEB cohort, the number of Americans living with cancer is projected to increase significantly by 2050 (to approximately 3 million persons) (25). Breast, prostate, lung, and colon cancer are the most frequently diagnosed cancers in the United States—and the risk increases with age. Meanwhile, the risk of dying from cancer is increased in African American and Latino "Boomers".

Remember the television commercials in the 1970s for Virginia Slims? This cigarette was the first to be solely marketed to women (26). Cigarette marketing to women in the 1970s was very effective, and diagnoses of lung cancer in women—low in the females of previous generations—are nearly equal to men in the "Baby Boomer" generation. According to the Centers for Disease Control, 110,322 males and 97,017 females were diagnosed with lung cancer in 2011 (and lung cancer is associated with the highest mortality) (27).

Meanwhile, one—out of every three—women gets breast cancer. At age 40, the risk of invasive breast cancer is actually one in 69 (but it increases after that age) (28). For men between the ages of 40-59, the risk of developing prostate cancer is one in 38—and men are 35 times more likely to develop prostate cancer than women to develop breast cancer (29).

African American and Latino "Boomers" in the LEB cohort have a lower survival rate for all of these cancers than white "Boomers". They are also less likely to have jobs that offer health insurance (since older African Americans and Latinos are disproportionately represented in low-wage employment).

As widely recognized, healthcare costs for cancer treatment are astronomical. In fact, medical debt is the largest single cause of personal bankruptcy. Therefore, acquiring and maintaining adequate health insurance is of prime importance to the LEB cohort.

Alzheimer's Disease

In the 2015 Hollywood movie—Still Alice—Julianne Moore plays a professor at 50 who learns that she has early Alzheimer's disease. While developing Alzheimer's disease at age 50 is unusual, it is a huge fear for "Baby Boomers". But, that fear is not only for themselves. Since Americans are living in large numbers into their eighties and nineties, more elders than ever are living with Alzheimer's disease (and other forms of dementia).

The burden of care for family members with Alzheimer's disease (and other forms of dementia) is falling heavily on female LEB "Boomers". In 2014, approximately 5.2 million Americans were living with Alzheimer's disease—and 200,000 were younger than age 65, according to the Alzheimer's Association. Additionally, two-thirds of these afflicted individuals are women (31).

Assisted living communities are not equipped to provide assistance to residents with dementia.

However, being moved from familiar surroundings exacerbates the memory problems associated with dementia—creating an untenable choice for "Boomer" offspring. All too often, the adult child or spouse of a person with Alzheimer's disease decreases work hours to spend more time with the afflicted person, which creates financial strain on the caregiver.

Housing Concerns and Needs

It cannot be overstated how concerned "Baby Boomers" are about housing in their old age. The problems inherent in seniors living alone—without adequate support—is a huge societal concern. The "graying" of our society is placing a huge strain on the next generation. As "Boomers" witness the difficulties faced by elders in their homes (especially after being diagnosed with a chronic disability), the LEBs are extremely anxious about how they will survive. Who will mow the lawn, and shovel snow from the sidewalk when they cannot do it? How will they get to appointments when they can no longer drive?

In this decade, there has been a huge spurt in 55+ housing developments—catering to "Boomers" who do not want to live with children. However, segregated housing by age can be problematic for this demographic in their so-called "golden years". Governmental intervention will be needed to meet the housing needs of "Boomers" once they reach old age.

Long-Term Care Insurance

The late 1970s saw the advent of long-term care insurance in the United States, and this industry came into its stride in the 1990s (in response to awareness of the costs of senior care) (30). While it can sound like a solution for "Baby Boomers" to meet the costs of home health, rehab care, and nursing home care in future, the cost of long-term insurance is prohibitive for many older people. Also, the future is actually unknown. Nevertheless, "Boomers" who have chronic conditions or a disability may benefit—at least psychologically—from purchasing this type of insurance.

As already mentioned, there is a looming crisis for "Baby Boomers" based on a lack of retirement savings, age-based employment discrimination, cost of health insurance, and lack of societal supports for seniors. No wonder so many "Boomers" are anxious about the future!

Economics, Governmental Policies, and "Boomer" Economics

Since 2000, the middle-class has been steadily shrinking in the United States, and income disparities have increased (31). But, the problem actually did not start in 2000. It started in 1981 under President Reagan when he threatened to fire striking air traffic controllers if they did not return to work. The "breaking" of the strike (called by Professional Air Traffic Controllers Organization [PATCO]) heralded a shift in governmental attitude toward labor unions. Collective bargaining had succeeded in improving the wages and benefits for industrial workers following World War II. In turn, their higher monthly incomes (and spending on goods and services) increased the strength of the economy—because consumer spending is vital for a healthy national economy.

Although the Recession was declared "over" in 2009, there is little debate that the employment rate is still sluggish as compared to before 2008 (and that pay has stagnated for most Americans). News articles are plentiful in reporting that CEO salaries have climbed dramatically since 2000, while the hourly wages for individuals without college degrees have fallen. Meanwhile, labor unions have been severely weakened in the past 20 years—both by state laws and decreased membership.

More than any other generation, LEB "Boomers" have been wounded by the loss of labor union clout—whether in the private or public sector. Those who had expectations of receiving a pension at retirement have found their hopes dashed. Others have had to drain their retirement accounts to pay for necessities after a "lay-off". Still others have had to defer dreams of retirement, because the Recession wiped out their assets.

This was a generation that was idealistic about the future, and that had a great deal of faith in the political process to achieve societal equality. At a time when they need most to attend to maintaining their physical and mental health, most "Boomers" are terrified of an impoverished future—while finding it difficult to curtail their spending.

Added to the pervasive anxiety about the future, the children of a large proportion of "Boomers" are not likely to attain the economic status of their parents—and they know it. The reason is that these young adults are absolutely swamped with college and credit card debit. In record numbers, these twenty-somethings are delaying the traditional milestones of adulthood—entering a marriage, starting a family, and purchasing a home. Yet, this lack of home-buying among "Millennials" is preventing the expansion of the national economy. It's a vicious cycle, leading to a downward spiral.

The wisdom and experience of "Boomers" feeds their anxiety for the future financial security of themselves and their offspring. But, government is not currently dealing with the looming crisis. Instead, the initiation of social programs to off-set the effects of a sluggish economy is left to nonprofit organizations, who are not capable of meeting needs formerly addressed by governmental entities.

The defining experience of "Boomers" at the current time is as "care-givers". Additionally, there are looming health issues for this cohort—and a huge need for healthcare practitioners and mental health counselors with training in gerontology. (As a field, this need is expected to drive the growth of educational programs in gerontology across many health-related careers.)

No organization in the United States has recognized the needs of "Baby Boomers"—and lobbied for governmental action on their behalf—as much as the American Association of Retired Persons (AARP). In 1999, AARP changed its focus from retired persons to all persons aged 50 or older. Likewise, it features numerous articles aimed at "Baby Boomers" in its bi-monthly magazine, called AARP The Magazine (with more than 47 million readers as of 2015).

Each issue of this magazine displays famous persons who are 50, 60, 70, and older (and who exemplify the possibility of enjoying an active, healthy, and fulfilling time in that decade of life). "Baby Boomers" may be invisible or devalued in popular media and culture, but they are still seeking ways to have new and exciting life adventures, and make a difference in the world around them. Don't count them out!

References

1)   Colby SL, and Ortman JM. (2014). The Baby Boom Cohort in the United States: 2012 to 2060; Population Estimates and Projections. United States Census Bureau: Washington, DC. Document # P25-1141. [Online report] Website: http://www.census.gov/prod/2014pubs/p25-1141.pdf

2)   Colby SL, and Ortman JM. (2014). The Baby Boom Cohort in the United States: 2012 to 2060; Population Estimates and Projections. United States Census Bureau: Washington, DC. Document # P25-1141. [Online report] Website: http://www.census.gov/prod/2014pubs/p25-1141.pdf

3)   Corporation for National and Community Service. Baby Boomer Volunteer Rates. [online] Website: http://www.volunteeringinamerica.gov/rankings/States/Baby-Boomer-Volunteer-Rates/2011

4)   Lewis, Kern. (November 9, 2012). Pick Baby Boomers as Your Target Market for the Holidays. Forbes [online article] Website: http://www.forbes.com/sites/kernlewis/2012/11/09/pick-baby-boomers-as-your-target-market-for-the-holidays/

5)   Songfacts.com. I'm a Woman, by Peggy Lee. [online Fact-Sheet] Website: http://www.songfacts.com/detail.php?id=16475

6)   Mayer, Gerald. (August 31, 2004). Union Membership Trends in the United States. Washington, DC: Congressional Research Service [online at Cornell University ILR School Digital Commons] Website: http://digitalcommons.ilr.cornell.edu/cgi/viewcontent.cgi?article=1176&context=key_workplace

7)   Mayer, Gerald. (August 31, 2004). Union Membership Trends in the United States. Washington, DC: Congressional Research Service [online at Cornell University ILR School Digital Commons] Website: http://digitalcommons.ilr.cornell.edu/cgi/viewcontent.cgi?article=1176&context=key_workplace

8)   Frugal Retirement Living.com. Baby Boomer Golf...A Growing Market. [online] Website: http://www.frugal-retirement-living.com/baby-boomer-golf.html

9)   Colby SL, and Ortman JM. (2014). The Baby Boom Cohort in the United States: 2012 to 2060; Population Estimates and Projections. United States Census Bureau: Washington, DC. Document # P25-1141. [Online report] Website: http://www.census.gov/prod/2014pubs/p25-1141.pdf

10)   Black Demographics.com. [online] Website: http://blackdemographics.com/population/

11)   Meyers, Bud. (August 26, 2013). Long-Term Unemployed Baby Boomers in 2013. The Economic Populist [online article] Website: http://www.economicpopulist.org/content/long-term-unemployed-baby-boomers-2013-5345

12)   Luo, Michael. (April 12, 2009). Longer Unemployment for Those 45 and Older. The New York Times [online article] Website: http://www.nytimes.com/2009/04/13/us/13age.html?pagewanted=all&_r=0

13)   Wealth Management.com. Here Come the Boomer Biz Owners. [online] Website: http://wealthmanagement.com/retirement-planning/here-come-boomer-biz-owners

14)   Immersion Active.com. Resources: 50+ Fact and Fiction. [online fact-sheet] Website: http://www.immersionactive.com/resources/50-plus-facts-and-fiction/

15)   Morgan, Carol, and Levy, Doran. (2002). Marketing to the Mindset of Boomers and Their Elders: Using Psychographics and More to Identify and Reach Your Best Targets. Attitude Base. ISBN-13 # 978-0970560513 and ISBN-10 # 0970560516

16)   U.S. Dept. of Health and Human Services; LongTerm-Care.gov. Costs of Care. [online fact-sheet] Website: http://longtermcare.gov/costs-how-to-pay/costs-of-care/

17)   Fry, Richard. (August 1, 2013). A Rising Share of Young Adults Live in Their Parents' Home. Pew Research Center [online article] Website: http://www.pewsocialtrends.org/2013/08/01/a-rising-share-of-young-adults-live-in-their-parents-home/

18)   Laidlaw K, and Paschana N. (2009). Aging, mental health, and demographic change: Challenges for psychotherapists. Professional Psychology: Research and Practice 40(6): 601-608.

19)   National Coalition for the Homeless. Homeless Veterans. [online fact-sheet] Website: http://www.nationalhomeless.org/factsheets/veterans.html

20)   Stevenson Betsey, and Wolfers, Justin. (2011). Trends in Marital Stability. In: Research Handbook on the Economics of Family Law. Lloyd Cohen and Joshua Wright (Editors). Edward Elgar: Northampton, MA and Cheltenham, UK. Website: http://users.nber.org/~jwolfers/Papers/TrendsinMaritalStability.pdf

21)   Bureau of Labor Statistics, U.S. Department of Labor. (November 8, 2013). Marriage and divorce rates among baby boomers vary by educational attainment. TED: The Economics Daily. [online] Website: http://www.bls.gov/opub/ted/2013/ted_20131108.htm

22)   Redfoot R, Feinberg L, and Houser A. (August 2013). The Aging of the Baby Boom and the Growing Care Gap: A Look at Future Declines in the Availability of Family Caregivers. American Association of Retired Persons, Public Policy Institute: Washington, DC.

23)   American Heart Association. Baby Boomers and Cardio-vascular Diseases. Statistical Fact Sheet 2013 Update. [online] Website: http://www.heart.org/idc/groups/heart-pub-lic/@wcm/@sop/@smd/documents/downloadable/ucm_319571.pdf

24)   MacMillan.org. Who Gets Cancer? [online] Website:
http://www.macmillan.org.uk/Cancerinformation/Aboutcancer/Who
getscancer.aspx

25)   Cancer-Research-Awareness.com. Baby Boomers Coming
Cancer Tsunami [online] Website: http://www.cancer-research-
awareness.com/baby-boomers-coming-cancer-tsunami.html

26)   Wikipedia. Women and Smoking. Webpage:
http://en.wikipedia.org/wiki/Women_and_smoking

27)   Centers for Disease Control and Prevention. Lung Cancer
Statistics. [online] Website:
http://www.cdc.gov/cancer/lung/statistics/

28)   BreastCancer.org. Risk of Developing Breast Cancer.
[online] Website:
http://www.breastcancer.org/symptoms/understand_bc/risk/under
standing

29)   Prostate Cancer Foundation. Prostate Cancer FAQs.
[online] Website:
http://www.pcf.org/site/c.leJRIROrEpH/b.5800851/k.645A/Prostate
_Cancer_FAQs.htm

30)   FreeAdvice.com. Law Advice: The History of Long Term
Care Insurance. [online] Website:
http://law.freeadvice.com/insurance_law/long_term_care/history-
of-long-term-care.htm

31)   Parlapiano A, Gebeloff R, and Carter S. (January 26,
2015). The Shrinking American Middle Class. New York Times
[online] Website:
http://www.nytimes.com/interactive/2015/01/25/upshot/shrinking
-middle-class.html?_r=0&abt=0002&abg=0

Resources

FREE! Five PULLING Email Autoresponders!!

Sign up for my newsletter and get five MLM generic email messages! You will get updates and ideas that you can use right away in your business, each week. No company is ever pitched, and you'll enjoy a bit of my humor as well. (maybe)

www.DavidWilliamsMLMAuthor.com

☐udio

The Fastest way to Networking Perfection: Rapid Business Hypnosis CD's and MP3 downloads. These are the ONLY Hypnosis CD's I recommend and use.

Rapid hypnosis success Vol 1

From my Desk:

Want to know the $9.99 tool that increased my production massively in one month? Sorry, but you can't buy it from me.

Now this tool has been out for just 3 years, but only a few clever networkers are sharing it with their team. However I have seen the results first hand – on myself – and my team – and I believe anyone in our industry who has not achieved their goals NEED's to use this simple, inexpensive and very effective 'unfair advantage'.

I remember just how I discovered these. It was a few years ago and I was frustrated with some negative attitudes that were showing themselves just after the 2008 crash. It was all over the TV, social media, the radio, every place you went. Times got tough and you could feel it.

I knew that no matter how strong our Mindset was, the negativity was going to attack us. And just like any army that is strong enough to withstand an attack it can still hurt!

I had an opportunity to do some consulting with a fellow who was an expert in the mind, and how to influence it by hypnosis and other techniques. I was approached to consult with the company that he chose to produce his CDs and audio downloads. They needed someone to write some advertising copy about his products for their sales page. I did not have time to take the contract, but I was totally convinced by all the science I saw.

They had titles that were about Abundance, Creating Wealth, Law of Attraction, etc. Even some about general sales. They offered me a few to try, but since I turned down their job offer, I felt better by paying for them.

I started with the Abundance and Wealth Creation hypnosis MP3s and after one week, I could 'notice' a difference.

The benefits really showed after the 4th week of use. Profound is not the word for it. I found that my production was up, and that meant more and more money. I could see the results in my bottom line - where results count!

I was also 'attracting' far better prospects, and I eliminated poor prospects faster. It was amazing. For me this was just so fantastic!

I did two things:

First I MADE (not asked) all of my team leaders to purchase their own copy, and use them.

Sure I could have copied mine – but I have learned from experience – things given for free are not used. Value must be felt by the user – and the best way to have them feel the value is for them to pay too. Don't forget this lesson.

Second I told the people behind these amazing hypnosis audios that they need to create some for the network marketing industry, and not just 'generalized' but very specific. I told them they need to deal with follow-up, 'the heavy phone syndrome', feeling negative about sales, seeking good prospects, Law of Attraction, etc. I gave them a big list!

They took my advice and set them up for sale online about 3 years ago for $39.99 for each album.

But NO! They are NOT $39.99!

I implored them to offer them on Apple and Amazon so all networkers could find them. I'm happy to say they did, (instead of their own site because they are now priced much less than $39.99). These powerful and life changing audios can be found on iTunes, Amazon MP3, Google Play, Beats Music, Spotify, Rhapsody, Emusic, & MediaNet for $9.99!

If you are in a rush, just search for "Rapid Hypnosis Success Network Marketing MP3" on Amazon or iTunes, Google Play etc. Get all 5 albums, or you can buy a few MP3s from each set for .89 cents each.

I'll give you a few links and titles – but first I just want to thank the good folks at Rapid Hypnosis Success for taking the time to research and create this program. When you hear them, you will know right away how powerful they will be for you.

These MP3's are on the iPads, iPods and other devices of not only me, but the key members of all of my teams. And while I am not 'active' anymore, I listen to at least one of them daily.

I decided it was high-time to share this secret advantage with everyone.

Sadly, I know many 'top dogs' who use these too, yet don't want anyone else to known about them. They are trapped in the 'old school' competition trap.

Ok, take a look at what you get on the first album Network Marketing Rapid Mindset Hypnosis Success - Volume 1 (There are 40 tracks on each album):

I Love Prospecting - Hypnotic Suggestions for Network Marketing Day 1

Become Persistent & Consistent - Hypnotic Suggestions for Networking Day 1

Eliminating the Fear of No's - Hypnotic Suggestions for Network Marketing Day 1

Winning Network Attitude - Hypnotic Suggestions for Network Marketing Day 1

Just go to your favorite online music story and search:

"Rapid Hypnosis Success Network Marketing"

Find and order all 5.

There are no affiliate links here – I'm giving this to you because I have really seen the positive change in – not only myself – but in entire teams, large groups, and at least one company who ordered them for each distributor.

So today, do your business a favor, invest in yourself and get a hold of this unfair advantage right now!

☐oo☐s☐

How to Brand Yourself for your Network Marketing Business: 9 Simple Steps to Explode your Business Using Easy, Simple Methods Online

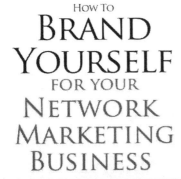

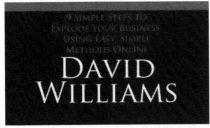

If you're a networker and want to find a way to close more business, to have more clout with cold market, if you want to stop sponsor-shoppers, and to close your prospects without the need of your upline, if you want to be more confident because your prospect is pre-sold on you, then this is YOUR BOOK!

Welcome to all the shortcuts, insider branding methods, and Internet secrets for pre-qualifying prospects that all the big names use, and you can too.

What is the difference between you and your successful upline?

Why is it your successful upline can take people through the process and you feel you can't?

The process is the same, the products are the same, it's all the same, except for one thing: you.

Why? Because, whether they know it or not, your upline styles themselves as an expert. Either consciously or unconsciously, they come across with authority and communicate from a position of strength. This is what you are going to learn and do. When you are the expert, your entire posture over the phone will change.

Why? Because when you know that your prospect is pre-disposed to believe and respect you - your phone delivery changes. Your prospect feels good about you, and feels privileged to follow you through the process. They might say 'no,' but it's a real no, a no after the process ends. But the more people you take entirely THROUGH the process, the more yes's you will have. Your closing rate will soar. Not only that, those 'no's' will stay in your autoresponder system longer now, and you'll be surprised that a few months later, they will turn into 'yes's'.

By being an 'expert' or authority, you will find building your business a charm, not a chore. When you follow what is outlined in this book, you will find people answer your phone calls, they call your conference call on time, attend your webinars, and follow up on your emails.

Why? Because in their eyes, you are a 'someone.'

Think of it this way: right now, prior to setting yourself up as an expert or an authority, you are floating in the ocean as one of a million other drops of water, each one saying the same thing, with the same scripts, same autoresponders, same replicated websites, same marketing material, trying to sell your prospect to join with YOU.

If they ask you, 'why should I join with you?' you'll say 'It's not about me, it's about you, and by the way, we have access to my upline who is Mrs. Big Shot, who is able to break the rules of physics and spread herself so thin she will promise to help you build your business too.'

OR....

...you are someone who has wisely invested in this book. You have decided to take matters into your own hands, and create a situation where your prospect is already sold on working with you. They will not ask 'how are you doing in the businesses' because they will assume that you are successful based on what they have seen; they will not even ask about upline support, because they will be looking at YOU as their mentor.

Even those with network experience will be impressed, and look forward to working with you. You will sound strong on the phone, and speak from a position of authority and strength, because you know you appear strong. Your prospects are impressed, will take your calls, follow up with you, and, for those who say no or disappear, you know it's not because they found someone 'better,' it's just that they are not interested or serious about changing their lives.

You'll find rejection disappears and struggling ends. Your value to your downline, your company, and to your prospects increases. And, as an expert, there is no more hard selling, closing becomes easy, and you become irresistibly attractive. If you are ready to become irresistibly attractive you're ready to Brand Yourself - order today and Get Started!

The Only Mindset Book You'll Ever Need for Network Marketing Success

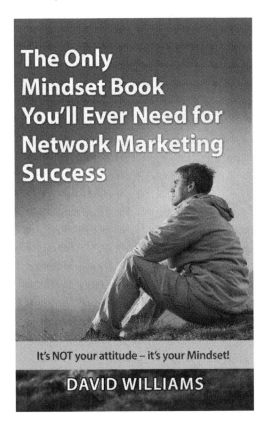

What would it be like...

To walk across the stage at your company's annual convention?

To be welcomed by your company's President as the newest top-level distributor?

How would it feel to have your spouse and family in the audience?

To never again hear "When are you going to get a real job?"

To be the leader you know you are, the example of how to be successful in this business, of finally reaching the top?

Can you achieve that?

Yes, with the right Mindset you can without any doubt.

PLEASE NOTE: This is NOT a book about 'Attitude'. This book zeroes-in on your Mindset.

How to Recruit Doctors into your MLM or Network Marketing team by showing them a NO Warm Market System

Where to Find Doctors – It's not where you think

A new source of Doctors (medical) who are not busy

Perfect for the Wellness Industry

No buying Leads

Not working the phone

This book is going to teach you an amazing system to recruit Doctors and an amazing system for you to build a huge, profitable and unstoppable leg under them - without the Doctor using any of their warm market, 'buying leads' or touching the phone!

Full Discloser: This is a short book. It's less than 50 pages long. It contains no fluff or padding. It's direct and to the point. The system contained is worth hundreds of thousands of dollars in sales, and could retire you. Really. Forget the low price of $8.99, forget the number of pages. This book will show you a fool proof system that ANY one can follow to build an unstoppable MLM Network Marketing business by recruiting Doctors. I have made it newbie friendly, but those with experience will take this system and put into practice very quickly.

This book will cover, step by step, and in very detailed and specific language:

The 'invisible' secret source of Doctors without a practice that are begging for something like what you will be able to show them

How to recruit busy Doctors with a practice and zero time

How to avoid the 'I don't want to go to my contacts/warm market' objection because you will be teaching them a system that requires ZERO warm market

And No 'buying leads'!

How to fill, yes FILL, meeting rooms with prospects all eager to join and try your products

NO conference calls, webinars, websites, Fanpages, autoresponders etc.

This is the full system, from the free ads you will place to the words on the marketing material you will print. This approached is very inexpensive to follow, quick and easy to implement, and very straight forward.

Also included are the phone scripts and person to person scripts you need to use when speaking to the Doctors, their receptionists, and to use in getting the appointment.

Forget all the 'usual suspects' techniques, this is not about dropping off DVDs, inviting them to conference calls, or creating special 'Doctors only' presentations. Forget all of that, and forget all of your old scripts and ads.

This system works for Doctors and requires NO Warm Market – I know I said that above, but it's very important you know this.

You don't need any paid advertising, Facebook, Internet, Twitter etc., this is all offline, local, and affordable.

No one has taught you this before. Guaranteed.

□□□ □cri□□ □reasur□□ No□ □our □sua□Ne□□or□ □ar□e□ng □□ne □cri□s

This book is full of the top pulling, most valuable and very rare MLM phone scripts that have earned their users many hundreds of thousands of dollars. I will say right now, the material in this book is NOT 'newbie' friendly. These scripts are for pros. If you don't know what you're doing this book is not for you.

Turn your prospects voice mail into a recruiting machine! 12 scripts which you can customize

What do I say to make sure my prospects watch's my DVD or online presentation?

What is a GAP line and why you should use one, and what to say on it

How to take your prospects pulse

Top Tier Phone scripts – rare and valuable – and great to modify for your own phone scripts

What to say to get your prospect on to a conference call

How to close your prospect after a conference call – lots of trial closes, hard closes, and objection handlers

Common objections and how to turn them back into closing questions

I have chosen scripts that I know you will NOT find in other script books for sale, or the free PDFs that float all over the Internet. The scripts contained here are the kind of scripts that only the top leaders in a program have access to and it usually requires someone to be invited to join their inner team to gain access to them.

-Scripts to get a prospect to commit to a live conference call

-The hardest closing questions from the industry

-Ads that will get your Voice Mail full, and what to say on your Voice Mail screener – lots of screeners and out bound messages

-What to say to your prospect AFTER the conference call

-Voice Scripts to 'wake up the dead' – get your inactive distributors active again

-Starting your own MLM or Team Call? Need a conference call script? – 4 full conference call scripts inside

-Are you a company trainer? Do you do many trainings? Are your people dying on the phone?

If you are a trainer, a serious upline, on your way to being a player, a 'big dog', this book is for you. If you are putting together your own scripts, calls, establishing your own team, or your own network marketing company – invest in this book. Inside this book you will find: hard hitting, hard closing power calls, what to say when you reach a prospects voice mail, screeners, actual company conference calls, GAP line messages and some special bonuses to get your phone ringing plus much, much more. It's all here.

What is in this book can take a serious player to the next level.

This is most definitely an 'insider's book'.

□□□ □u□res□onder □essages and Ne□□or□ □ar□e□ing □□ai□□essages□ □inancia□□ oes □ac□

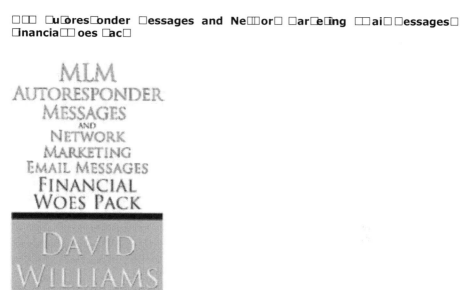

This book contains a professionally written email drip campaign of 30 powerful, engaging and entertaining persuasive email/autoresponder messages focused on your prospects 'Financial Woes' and how YOU can help your prospect solve them.

Warning!

If you have been in Network Marketing for any length of time, you probably have accumulated a list of prospects and their email address. However, many of these prospects have entered the 'witness protection program'. In other words, they never call back or reply to your emails. Most people forget about this list, but there is GOLD in it!

Now, you probably have an email system you pay for that is filled with 'canned' autoresponders about your company, or even some generic versions to send to your list. Some-times this is part of your 'back-office'.

But, have you read these autoresponders being sent in your name?

They're terrible!

Here's why:

You have a prospect who is looking to solve THEIR problem, which is lack of money. They need money, income, some light at the end of the tunnel, cash, maybe some dough to save their home... BUT they are NOT shopping for a MLM company, an

INDUSTRY, or how long your company has been in business, or even what your product does...NO... they are desperate for a SOLUTION to their problems!

But if all the emails you send out are about 'the company, the timing, the industry...or how someone else is making money' – no wonder they don't bother responding to you!

Your prospect doesn't care about other people's wealth when THEY are broke and in financial pain. In fact, it works the other why. Resentment, suspicion, distrust.

Their mind is on their lack of money and they are worried.

They are awake all night worrying about their debt because they are in financial trouble.

And what? You send them an email about how old your company is?

It's basic marketing; offer your prospect a solution to their problem, and relate to them on their terms.

So, what is in this book? Do I teach you how to write emails? NO...NO...and NO!!!!

Is this some lessons on basic copy writing for MLM? Heck NO!!!

But let's face it. Most people can't write a note to save their lives, let alone a well-crafted email campaign. Forget learning a skill that will take you years to master – just use expert messages instead!

That's where this book of powerful 'financial woes' autoresponder messages will come to your aid.

Inside are 30 rock solid emails that focus on your prospects financial situation - with engaging humor and playfulness - showing how YOU and your program can help him out of his or her financial mess.

FULL DISCLOSURE – this is a small book – 30 powerful emails. You are not paying for the quantity of words, you are paying for the quality of the message and for getting your phone to ring.

This book contains 30 well-crafted powerfully written emails that and fun and engaging that will suggest and reinforce to your prospect that YOU are the answer to their financial problems using proven psychological and persuasion techniques.

Take these email autoresponder messages and enter them into your back-office or your email program. Start dripping on your list with these professionally written email messages – each crafted to have your prospect motivated to reach out and call YOU as an answer to their Financial Woes!

□□□ □u□res□onder Ne□□or□□ar□e□ng □□ai□□essages□□ e□ñess Nu□ri□iona□ □ac□

This is a completely different set of email messages then those in the above book. You can add these to the 30 in the above book, or use them on their own. However they are written just for networkers in wellness programs.

From the Description:

This book contains a professionally written email drip campaign of 30 powerful, engaging and entertaining persuasive email/autoresponder messages focused on the wellness industry.

If your products include wellness, nutritional or related products, this drip list campaign will engage your prospect and have them calling you. These autoresponder messages contain humor, personality, and are wellness/health/nutritional related.

They are perfect for the person who appreciates wellness or nutrition as a cause AND a vehicle for profit. It assumes that your prospect likes to 'help' people and has an interest in

Interest in seeing their level of health improved.

Deregulation and Energy MLM Email Prospecting Autoresponder Messages: for Network Marketing companies offering Electricity or Natural Gas

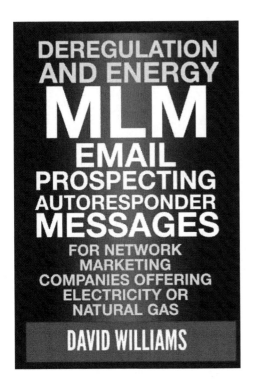

This book contains a professionally written email drip campaign of 30 powerful, engaging and entertaining persuasive email/autoresponder messages focusing on the Energy industry.

These emails are perfect for North American Power, 5Linx, Veridian, CCM Consumer Choice Marketing, Momentis, IGNITE, Ambit, ACN - and any other energy or electricity network marketing company.

If your products include electricity, natural gas or related products, this drip list campaign will engage your prospect and have them calling you.

These autoresponder messages contain humor, personality, and are energy and deregulation related. They are perfect for the person who looking for a REAL residual income.

Each email ends with asking the prospect to call you now as the call to action.

Ho☐ ☐o ☐ros☐ec☐and ☐ecrui☐using ☐os☐ards ☐r ☐our ☐☐ or Ne☐☐or☐ ☐ar☐e☐ng ☐usiness ☐☐e ☐o☐ cos☐ros☐ec☐ng and ☐ecrui☐ng ☐o☐☐a☐☐u☐ ☐er☐or☐s ☐n☐he ☐e☐☐ods

HOW TO
PROSPECT
AND RECRUIT
USING
Postcards
FOR YOUR MLM OR
NETWORK MARKETING BUSINESS

The Low Cost Prospecting and Recruiting Tool that Out Performs Online Methods

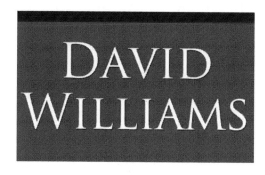

DAVID
WILLIAMS

Fed up not having quality leads?

Are you in a MLM company you love, but just can't find REAL prospects to talk to?

Tried 'online' leads but found you just wasted your time and money?

Many networkers are well past the 'warm market' stage, and are struggling to find success. It seems the entire world has gone online and the problem that networkers face is sticking out in an ever increasing ocean of websites, mobile apps, opt-in forms, blog posts, Face-book Likes, YouTube movies and Tweets. It never ends.

There is alternative. There is another way.

Because the world HAS gone online, good old fashioned Direct Mail is making a comeback. Why? Because no one gets 'real' mail anymore. You have zero competition!

And what's more real than a picture postcard?

NOTE:

What This Book is NOT about: this book in no way teaches you to send those ugly, tacky, pre-printed, glossy pictures of fast expensive cars or mansions, or YELLOW 'print your own' postcards. NO, NO, NO!

If you are engaged in postcard marketing, buying glossy tacky 'in your face' MLM style postcards and mailing them out – or worse – paying to have them mailed out – I'll show you a method that will increase your success by a massive amount – because I guarantee your message will be read if you use the method I teach.

Or, if you are prospecting with one of those 'print your own' cards at the local Office Max, mailing out thousands until you're broke by sending ugly cards – you will be so happy switching to my method because it will save you time, money, you'll mail out less cards and get massive more results.

Again, because I guarantee your prospect will read your message.

I will show you a method that combines two of the most important recruiting factors for success in MLM:

Mass Recruiting and Personalization

And NO – this is not about using computer 'hand writing fonts'!!!

I'll show you a method to recruit massively with postcards, in a very personalized way for your prospect to find it impossible to not read your message and make a call.

This works. This book is based on my famous Direct Mail for Networkers seminars that were part of a $10,000 MLM insider's weekend training. You will get this same information for less than $10. And the best part of it is, this system works even better today than before! Why? Because the power of a postcard, personalized, is stronger today in this Internet age.

Full Disclosure: This is a short, to the point book. It's not full of padding or fluff, (however, I do trace for you how I discovered my introduction into Direct Mail for MLM Recruiting by a presidential fundraiser).

It's a 'How To' book. You are paying for the system, the magic, and the fact that you won't need any other information to get started.

I have included low or no budget methods as well.

Please NOTE: This book is for MLM or Network Marketing recruiting – it's not about post-card 'marketing' for non-MLM business. The information here is for network marketers who want to build downlines and offer a system to their team that does not rely on 'buying leads' from the internet and telemarketing 'survey leads', 'real time leads', 'fresh leads', or any of the other scammy descriptions of absolutely terrible leads for sale by lead companies.

Looking for a Low cost, but highly efficient network marketing tool way to get REAL leads? This is it.

□□□ and Ne□□or□□ar□e□ng □ro□essiona□s guide □□ □ecrui□ng □ e□□ess□and Ho□is□ic □rac□□oners □or □□□□□□e □ e□□ess □ndus□r□Hand□bo□□or □□□□ding □□ur □o□n□he

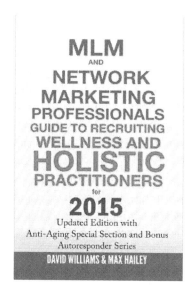

By David Williams and Max Hailey

This book was written for you because you need to learn how to take advantage of 2015 - two years where there will be a MAJOR jump forward in the Wellness MLM industry.

Miss these steps and you will regret it. Check out just some of the Table of Contents:

Who and How to Recruit How to Brand yourself on the net Holistic Wellness:

The new Holy Grail Recruiting ground - if you do it right How to turn this 'Holistic' trend into a downline exploding movement

Wellness: The answer to the Health Crisis and an Engine for Income behind Network

Marketing Sharing of Wellness: Why Network Marketing The REAL reasons why Wellness has Become More Profitable for the Networker

How to create a Product Zealot

How to use the Increase of Baby Boomers and Active Older Adults to light a fire in your recruiting

Where to find Boomers Targeting the Fitness and Weight Loss Market 9 Reasons

Why Obesity will fatten your bank account

Why Leading with the Product is Insanely Bad advice

The 2 Words That Will Make Wealth for the Network Marketer

The 9 Key Wellness categories - Where is the money for Networkers

And much more...

The Big Money One of most important (and in turn, one of the most profitable) industries in the United States today is the wellness industry. The wellness industry touches almost everyone around the world, so it's no wonder that the industry continues to grow.

This book will show you the wellness trends that you as a networker need to know, and how to take advantage of those. It will show you new and fertile recruiting grounds, as well as retail product sales markets. Included are Action Steps for 2015 listing what you need to do to develop your wellness networking business to take it to the top.

That's why you need this book.

Because what you'll learn will give you and your team more than a slight edge, you'll get a great leap forward. Because it will show you where and how to recruit in the Wellness industry. Once you understand your industry, by just using some of the facts in this book or the terminology, you'll be able to master the conversation, write effective presentations, deliver great testimonials and recruit 'up'. You'll be able to sign up wellness professionals and build a rock solid organization of real believers and not a bunch of mlm junkies.

In short, you'll find long term income and success. Imagine recruiting from people who already are pre-sold on what you do. It's like fishing from a stocked pond.

The information in this book will provide you with REAL reasons for being in the Wellness industry so you can dominate your prospecting and keep your team excited when they hit those emotional road blocks.

Recruiting: it will show you where to find prospects who are ready to start and who are already excited by wellness products. It will show you how to approach them, what to say, and the biggie, what NOT to say!

Lastly, the book will provide you with Action Steps of what to do to ride the wave of wellness.

1) Create your Internet content with information from this book to brand yourself

2) Use this information to educate & excite your prospects and new distributors

3) Find product zealots by sampling to targeted groups as shown here

4) Recruit Holistic practitioners - people already committed to Wellness

This is an invitation to wealth. You can't help but get rich if you take action now and build in 2015.

Read MLM and Network Marketing professionals guide to Recruiting Wellness and Holistic Practitioners for 2014 The Wellness Industry Handbook for Exploding your Downline

TODAY!

The □i□ □□s□□or□s□□os□b□er□□□□ and Ne□□or□□ar□e□ng □ros□ec□ Con□o□and C□sing □nes and □cri□□

Do you have trouble closing prospects? Do you feel you lose control of your prospecting and follow up calls? Do you have trouble closing strong prospects – the very ones you desperately want on your team?

Well, this book is for you. It's the lowest price but highest value book on Amazon. Why? Because this little book contains over 120 of the strongest, easiest, subtlest closing and 'keeping control' and 'taking control' over the conversation lines for network marketers.

FULL DISCLOSURE: This is a short book. This book has over 150 'lines'; mostly one line sentences. But don't be fooled by the size of the book. These are powerful closing lines to allow you to close your prospect. This is NOT a book on prospecting, recruiting or even a script book.

This is a book that should be open at your desk as you make your prospecting and follow up calls. If you find you prospect off their script (they never stay on script – only you can do that), these lines will bring you back into control.

They are subtle, but powerful. Here's some samples:

How much does it cost?

Millions of dollars not to get involved

Can you see yourself taking people through a process just like I did with you?

You can't outsource your learning

The table's set

This is thick

I'm not claiming we have an automatic system, I'm demonstrating it

Get into the game with us

Let me layout how the business will start for you

This is just a process to see if there a fit for you

This is not a pressure gig

It's just the way we do this (process)

There's no glory in paying bills

I promise I'm not going to push you, chase you or sell you

I'm not going to come back to close you, but to personalize the business for you

NOTE: with very little modification, you can use many of these lines as ad headers, email subject lines, or as smart and directed text in emails or create new phone scripts or reinvigorate old ones.

If you lose control of a conversation, or have a strong person on the line (the best kind to recruit), these 'lines' are the arrows in your quiver.

Make these lines your own. They have been collected by professionals and have earned those who have used them millions of dollars, no exaggerating, millions of dollars. Now for .99 cents they are yours.

This book of powerful network marketing closing and control lines provides you with the easiest way to sound strong on the phone. You just need to use them. You need to sound strong. Your prospect will never know what hit them until you are training them, and tell them to pick up this little book.

About the Author

If you want to know one thing about David Williams it's this:

He believes in OFFLINE prospecting and ONLINE follow up!

David Williams has been a top earner and top performer in networking for over 25 years. He has worked all over the world building teams successfully. In the last five years he has worked with corporations to develop MLM opportunities as well as top performers to create recruiting systems for their teams.

He also delivers 'insider only' high priced seminars for 'the big dogs' on practical MLM: prospecting, recruiting and team expansion.

Prior to Networking Williams' background was a few years of university – which meant he was broke.

In 2012 he decided to put into book-form some of the trainings he has done and offer them to anyone. Typically his work spreads word-of-mouth and word-of-mouse. Williams decided to present his insiders training at price levels that are affordable via the Internet to anyone but is not trying to disrupt the high priced seminars business either. Rather he feels that his readers are new and future leaders who are not even aware of these insider events but will one day will be seated there if they follow his systems.

Williams is not actively working any MLM program but enjoys 8 different residual income sources and in multiple currencies.

His favorite MLM tips include:

Fire your Upline

Be the Upline you want

Never stop recruiting

How much money would I make today if my downline did what I did?

He hates 'fluff' training.

He writes a MLM email training letter that he sends weekly - you can sign up for it at www.DavidWilliamsMLMAuthor.com

Those who have signed up for David's newsletter may reach him via that email address.

Feel free to contact him with any question.

DavidWilliamsAuthor@gmail.com

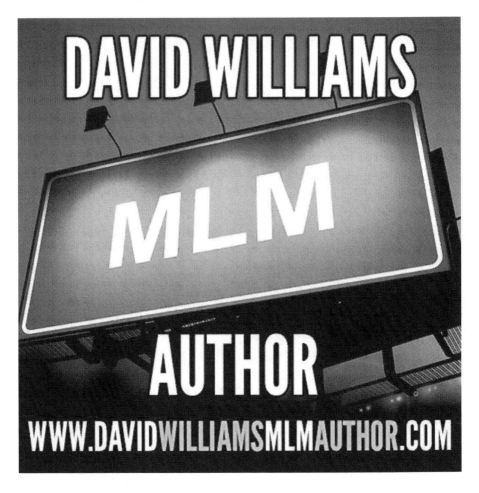

Made in the USA
San Bernardino, CA
01 December 2015